GW00865954

# A Letter To My Daughter

Life Experiences of
a World War II P.O.W.

by

# Frank Gill

*AuthorHouse™*
*1663 Liberty Drive, Suite 200*
*Bloomington, IN 47403*
*www.authorhouse.com*
*Phone: 1-800-839-8640*

*©2008 Frank Gill. All rights reserved.*

*No part of this book may be reproduced, stored in a retrieval system, or transmitted by any means without the written permission of the author.*

*First published by AuthorHouse 7/18/2008*

*ISBN: 978-1-4343-9041-7 (sc)*

*Printed in the United States of America*
*Bloomington, Indiana*

*This book is printed on acid-free paper.*

# One day in the life of a
# POW in Europe World War 2

*A day spent working at a quarry in Sudationland*

The guards would unlock the doors at 5-30am. Start blowing
a whistle as loud as possible. Shouting. "Up, Up Englander!"
If you did not respond immediatey they would use the rifle
butt to force you out.

   The only means of having a wash was a single, cold water
tap in the yard which had barbed wire around so you could not
escape.The latrines were also out tin the yard. There would be a
big tub full of what was called "Mint Tea" with no real taste, but
it was HOT! Nothing to eat since the night before when you had
got a piece of bread about the size of a slice of cake. This had to
last you all day.

   Around 6 a.m. the guards blew the whistle again.
This meant you had to go out into the yard. The walk to the
quarry took about an hour or so, through the village and then
up the hills. The work consisted of breaking up stones with a
very large, heavy hammer and then loading them onto a skip to
be transported to the factory to make lime. This work went on
all day whatever the weather! With only a half hour lunch break
but no lunch! There were two guards to twenty POW's.

   We finished at 5 p.m. or whenever it became dark. No
prisoners out at night in case we escaped! When we arrived at
the billet, we had a cold wash, then a big tub of "so-called" stew.
Mostly water, with a few potatoes with skins on and maybe a
few veg. Ones share would hardly fill a bird let alone a growing
youth. But that is how life had to be as a POW.

   We would spend the evening chatting or playing cards.
Go to bead around 8:00 or 9:00 then wake up in the middle of
the night with stomach pains due to hunger. Another day would
soon come around and life would be just the same routine.

   Roll on home!

# A word of dedication
## from your three daughters
*January 2008*

This story is an account of one man's life. Yet it represents the stories of many people who lived through The Second World War. These brave young men and women , with a belief and dedication, were willing to fight for future generations and I am proud to say that this man is my Dad. I want to say "Thank you" to you and all those who gave my family and I a future .

Your Loving Daughter.
Patricia. x.


What started off as a very personal memoir is now a fitting tribute to the bravery and perseverance of someone I am proud to call Dad. This book will be read through generations and I am privileged to have known the author not only as parent but above all as my best friend.

Your Loving Daughter.
Lorraine. x


I vividly remember a summer's Sunday in the mid Sixties, when I was alone and thoughtful and you came into our living room to join me.

I always knew that you had been a Prisoner of War and had been involved in The Second World War. It just seemed the right time to ask you.

"Dad! What was it like in The War?"

You began to relate some of the times and hardships that you subsequently went on to write in this wonderful book.

For many years after that day I carried those accounts in my heart and it was when I was teaching in South America that I knew I needed to hear more and so it was the time to ask you to write your life story.

This is, indeed, a wonderful achievement and a jewel for our future generations

Your Loving Daughter.
Helen. x

# Introduction

This story of my life, and the title, came to be because of a letter sent to me by my second daughter, Helen, upon her return from carrying out her profession as a teacher in South America in the early 1980's. The content of the letter read as follows;

Dad.

You know all about my life. Yet I do not know all about yours. I want you to sit down and write everything that has happened to you in all your 65 years. I know you suffered many hardships, many setbacks and many sad times. I'm sure, as well, there were abundant happy times. Many proud moments and memories that stand out vividly in your mind.

Tell me about these things, Dad, so I can keep them forever and treasure them always perhaps under the title of; "A Letter To My Daughter"

Who could resist an invitation such as that!! So, sit back and read on.

Frank Gill

*Helen aged 18 months. 1954*

# To My Daughter Helen

*Contents*

## *Chapter 1*
# Family

I was born on 26th July 1919. Baptised Frank Joseph. My parents were; Lucy Claire O'Rielly and Thomas Joseph Gill. The happy event took place at 19, Gainsborough Road, Toxteth, off Smithdown Road, Liverpool. England.

I had an elder sister, Eileen and two brothers. Both born after me. Unfortunately, Sean who was born on 12th July 1922, died before his first birthday from Meningitis.

Jack was born in Waterloo on 13th April 1933. A late comer but a welcome member. This completed our family. My Father who was born in Dublin on 7th July 1888, was a Master Mariner by profession, having gone to sea when aged 13. Before his first voyage was completed, both his Mother and Father had died. He served his time on the old sailing ships before moving into steam.

He passed his Masters Certificate of Competency on 17th May 1913. This Certificate entitled him also to serve as First Mate on Square Rigged Sailing Vessels. Quite an achievement, for he was only aged 25 at the time.

My Mother, also born in Dublin, on 8th August 1890, did not work after their marriage which took place in the Parish of Bray, Co. Dublin, on 26th June 1915.

My sister was born the following year, 1st September 1916. We traveled between Ireland and England many times during my early life and my first memories as a child are of living on the outskirts of Dublin.

Funnily enough two incidents which linger in my mind are of pain. First. When I knelt on a poker which I had taken out of the fire purposely to make a hole in a cupboard door. I lay the poker down, turned away, then back, and damage done. Mind you Helen, I don't think I should have been doing that sort of thing anyway. Perhaps it served me right!

I recall getting a ride on top of a bread-van. In those days the driver used to travel on the top of the van and drive the horses from that position. I was at my Auntie Alice's home, (my Mother's sister) which was a tree covered area from house to road. Now, as Eileen and I and the Driver traveled down that track an over hanging branch hit me in the throat. Fortunately I did not fall off as the Driver grabbed me, but I did suffer a lot of pain and, of course, lost my voice for a long time. Needless to say I did not ride on that van ever again.

I remember once being in a cupboard underneath the stairs in a cousin's house. There were about six of us altogether jumping around and acting the fool, when lo and behold, the whole lot collapsed on top of us.

Who was to blame? I don't know, but there was a big row about it and I don't think we went there again. I remember in my cousin Marie's home, jumping from a bed into a wooden box that was used for storing toys.

The game went well until my sister, Eileen, jumped but missed and fell head down catching a protruding nail just above her eye!!! Panic once more. I think the mark is there to this day as is mine from the poker.

My sister will tell the tale of me always pinching and biting her. But that I suppose was because, being three years older, she most likely bossed me around a lot. You'll note I don't deny it. Still we were good friends and our childhood together was mostly memories of fun and laughter.

We did live in Barrow-in-Furness (Northern England) for a short spell when my Dad was Assistant Harbour Master, but I don't remember that at all. I must have been very little. I don't recall my school days while living in Ireland. I did go to school there, but it must have been my first commencement of education and maybe I just didn't want to remember those experiences.

What does linger with me was the picnics we used to go on in Ireland. A Mr. O'Neil had a car and we would all pile in, set off to the country and enjoy ourselves singing songs on the way. Songs like, "Mow-A-Meadow," It could go on for as long as you wished. Good fun guy-that Mr O'Neil, Helen. Must have been rich to have owned a car in those days. If my memory serves me right, I think he was a school teacher. Now how about that! A teacher. Just like you!

Visiting my Uncle Jack, a step-brother of my mother, (He was a Priest and later became a Canon) was always a joy for us. Whenever we went he would always give us pocket money as well as a few questions on our faith, but we didn't mind the questions as we knew what would come later!

Looking back, I'm sure my Mum enjoyed being over in Ireland as all her family and friends were there, where as in England, she had to make and find friends herself.

When we came back to England we lived in an apartment off Upper Parliament Street. Mulgrave Street to be exact. At that time it was a respectable area and we played mostly in Princes Road where the trams ran down the centre of this very wide and quiet thoroughfare. The people that owned the house we lived in were very nice and became good friends of the family, but like everything else we lost contact with them as time went by and we moved on. It was not long before we moved out to Allerton. This area was nearer to Garston Docks where my Father docked upon his return from voyages at sea.

We lived at 82, Redington Road, an area where my life took on a different meaning. An area which brings back so many happy memories to to me. Even now when I drive through that part of Liverpool I relive those days of our childhood and joys. By the way Helen our Auntie Alice was also a school teacher! What do you know about that!

## Chapter 2
# Growing up

Both Eileen and I started school in Allerton, at the Catholic School in Garston, but as it was about twenty minutes walk, and remember ,we did not have buses to take us or bikes to ride there, we more often than not were soaked and spent the days sitting in class in wet clothes, ending up with cold after cold till in the end my Mother, who herself suffered the same soakings, as she used to take us to and bring us home, decided enough was enough and we went to a Church of England school near to our Corporation home.

*Photo of the author at age 7, Circa 1926*

Of course there were many problems for my Mother to bear because of the school change, but to her our health came first. I attended Springwood Junior and recall winning a big story book for finishing in the top three in my class.

My first prize and was I proud. I kept that Book for years, but in the end, out it went like many other things that contain memories. As a matter of fact it was the one and only award for study that I obtained during my long schooling years. Eventually I moved to the senior school of Heath Road, while Eileen attended Duncombe Road School for Girls. I played football for that school and enjoyed my period there.

Allerton was a lovely area for growing up and, as I say, I have many happy memories of a fine gang of playmates from those days. We used to run for miles, hitting a hoop in front of us with a new winner each time. We would go onto the Golf Course and pinch the balls as they came over the hill and the player could not see the hole. We would later sell those golf balls for sweet money. We used to camp out in the many fields round and about.

I recall my sister and I with an old sheet wrapped around a couple of sticks. Walking behind each other with the sticks on our shoulders, heading for a camping site and a grand day out together.

My cousin, Marie, used to accompany us when she was over on holiday and did we have fun? Yes, Helen. There was no doubt this place was perfect for growing up. Every day brought new adventures and a lot still remembered as you see. Our gang used to dig out big holes in the ground. Cover them with tin, timber and leaves, spending hours inside, especially if it was raining. Also we would appoint the leader of the gang by lighting a fire inside and who ever could stay in the smoke the longest was The Boss! It would be frowned on today I guess.

We used to climb the high wall running around the field area, see who could stay up the longest when the Policeman came along on his bike, drawing his baton and threatening us.

We considered that fun until the wall about 50 yards from our exploits with the Bobby was knocked down when a big tree was blown down during a gale, hence we knew he could possibly catch us so we stopped that episode!

The one draw back for me was the fact that when ever I went out with my pals my Mum would say. "Take Eileen with you and look after her."

That was a bind to me and held me back a lot, but although I was not keen, I remember getting into fights to protect my sister when any insults flew about.

My Mother was a wonderful person. She was also Father to us due to my Dads many long absences. She was never a really healthy female. Suffering mainly from Rheumatism. At times she was in great pain. This though did not stop her from giving us a wonderful, happy up -bringing. When we were little she would sit with us in front of the fire reading stories and playing games. I remember when the story of Alice In Wonderland was read. I used to cry. Silly me!

I used to look forward every day to my Mum reading "The Adventures of Rupert Bear" from the Daily Express Newspaper. Every time I see him now, my mind wonders back over those years.

Many games, apart from Ludo and Snakes and Ladders, were played with the poker and fire hob. We would see how many patterns we could spot in the flames and tell a thought up story about them. Remember Helie, no TV in those days and we had to be kept amused somehow.

While outside my Mum taught us to ride bicycles. Walking up and down Mather Avenue day after day holding the saddle until in the end success was ours. Such patience she had! My Mum taught us to respect people and property, to be honest, truthful and kind. She lead by example, never lost her temper and Lord knows there must have been many times when she should have done! Never, to my knowledge did she hit any of us, except, I must admit, that one time while we three were sat in front of the fire making toast and I kept pulling Eileen's hair,

I was told to stop a number of times but carried on and my Mum ,who had the bread knife in her hand struck out and the knife caught my ring finger on my left hand. Blood poured from it and we all panicked! Especially Mum who was so upset it had happened at all! I have that mark to this  day and it was all my fault.

Looking back,we adored our Mother but I wonder  if we showed it enough? I doubt it for we take everything for granted when young. My lasting memories over the years as regards my Mum are sad indeed as you will see later on. Tears come into my eyes even now as I write.

Growing up in Allerton was great. A lovely area and so much to do. I used to watch Springwood play football each Saturday. Also Cheshire Lines, whose ground was only a short distance away. We would go to the morning pictures shown at the Garston Empire on a Saturday. We looked forward to following the western serials week in, week out. Always about Cowboys and Indians shooting up the place! On the way home we had a favoured pastime I recall, of becoming those heroes and villans we had just marvelled at on the Big Screen!

I recall going on a couple of sea voyages with my Dad. This was when he was with the Coast Lines Company. He used to run between Liverpool,Cardiff and Ireland.

On one trip, the weather was pretty bad, blowing a gale and the ship was rolling all over the place. Needless to say I was sick .But while sitting in my Dad's cabin I started to eat through a packet of Water Biscuits and that seemed to cure me. I was never again sick and we did have some rough trips believe me. These sea trips were during school holidays and did give my Mum a break from coping on her own all the time. She, with Eileen, also came on a trip now and again but not a lot.
Life was good at this period. School was good. Everything was

fun and I was really happy. But alas, the joys of childhood have a habit of ending when least expected and that's exactly what happened. But before I go on with this letter to you dear Helen, I must first tell you about our pal, Peter, the dog that we had when in Allerton. We'd had dogs before. One when we lived in Wallasey, but it died from distemper when only a few months old.

Now Peter was something special. He grew up with us and became a real member of the family. He would follow us all over the place when we were out playing. He would get a half house brick, scratch it with his paws and lick it continually then carry it home when we returned.

At night he would play with Eileen and I. We would put him outside the room, then hide something and let him in. Where upon he would sniff around until, at last, he would find it with great shouts of joy from us all!

Then we'd play school with him. Eileen and I would stand in a separate corner of the room and Peter would be laying in front of the fire, but as soon as we would creep out he would jump up and rush us back into the corner---going from one to the other keeping us trapped in our respective spaces, This could go on for hours at a time. He brought much fun and joy to us all.

My Dad had a Brother who lived in New Zealand. He owned a lot of sheep on a big farm. Well, he died and although he had a wife and children he left all his money to my Dad. I never knew just how much it all was, but I do remember the wife making a claim through the Courts and winning an amount for herself and each of the children. It still left a fair amount for our family. Dad decided to give up the sea, mainly, I think because of Mother's continual ill health. This was a difficult decision for him as his whole life and love was for ships and the sea.

He, first of all bought a small car. A Morris Eight. It was always a nightmare driving around, for my Father, to say the least, was not the best of drivers, bearing in mind that in those days Driving Tests had not even been thought of and one could buy a car one day and take it on the road the next. At first I used to hide my head under a pillow in the back of the car. I recall one day in Liverpool, my Dad shot out from a side street in Church Street, almost hitting a tram car. Then almost through Marks and Spencers store window. Fortunately the car stalled and we were stuck in the middle of the road for ages!!! The language was hot from all sources as you can guess.

Some months later we were involved in an accident in Southport. I must admit it was not my Dad's fault. A Ribble Bus coming from the left hit the front right side of our car coming out of a side road. The car was a wreck and we all suffered injuries. Only slight Thank God! I had, by this time, ventured into the front passenger seat. Either my Dad was becoming a better driver or I had got used to the scares and didn't give a dam. I had dispensed with the pillow anyway! The result was that I broke my left arm. My Mum and sister had cuts. All had shock and we ended up in Southport Infirmary.

My Dad, who had a knock on the head did not, at the time, seem too bad .But later the wound, treated by a local district nurse, turned septic. Due mainly because she had advised him to wash his head every day and the infection ran into his eyes, ears etc. Ending up with him being admitted into Bootle Hospital where he remained for a number of weeks. They had to shave all his hair off. That must have been painful.

Prior to my Dad's hospitalisation, with the help of a friend who owned a poultry farm in Woolton, my Father bought his own Poultry Farm in Maghull. Hence, I had to leave Allerton with the rest of the family and that was a sad farewell. I shed many a tear after moving, for that place was to me, perfect.

The farm brought a complete new outlook to life. There were hundreds of hens and incubators full of chicks which were taken to market in Wales to be sold. I would clean and feed the fowl,and pick the apples and pears, when in season. They also went to market with the eggs.

I started school in the country village Catholic school of Saint Georges. Only a few children attended for Maghull, at that time, was a real country village. Many pranks did we get up to in that school. One in particular I remember was when one of the two teachers was off ill and the clock stopped. I was asked to loan my watch to the substitute teacher. Before doing so, I put it on about fifteen minutes which meant we got out of school that much earlier. However, I forgot to reset the watch and the following day we waited for the sweet shop to open at one o clock, which meant we were late for class and so the game was up. I blamed the watch, not myself!

I found a paper delivery round and used to, after the house deliveries, go to the Ministry of Pensions Hospital each evening. This is now Park Lane High Security Holding Hospital for the mentally and criminally ill. The men in the Pension Hospital were all First World War Veterans suffering from brain damage due to injuries at "The Front." They would black-out at anytime and I got to know a lot of them and got used to their unfortunate disabilities.

There were many concerts held in the hospital and I would stay to watch most of them. The inmates would wait for me at the gate and, many times, one or another of them would collapse in a fit! Sad it was. Little did I know at that time that I, myself, would be involved in a war. Just as well I suppose.

I got to know a lot of local lads and we formed a football team to play the surrounding villages. I made many friends, both male and female. Apple pinching was a favoured pastime, as long as they were not from my father's farm! There was little to do in Maghull especially in the winter months. It was a dead hole to say the least.

It was my father's intention to send me to a Boarding School to further my education. He chose Saint Joseph's College, Blackpool. All was arranged. I had been to the College for interview and was due to start at the beginning of the next term.

Now, at the paper shop where I was working, there was about four other lads and, of course, whenever the chance arose we would pinch chocolate or cigarettes. Unfortunately, the owner realised what was going on and caught us outside the shop with contraband in hand. He phoned around each boys' home and, of course, not only was that the end of my paper round, my Father also informed me that he would see that I was brought up correctly at home as I had drifted away from the teachings of my Mother. He immediately canceled my intended place at Saint Joseph's College. (I was pleased at that!) He arranged a place for me at Saint Mary's College, Crosby, a day school founded and run by Jesuit priests. Hence my higher education commenced.

I would have to leave home each morning at 7-30 am to catch a train from Maghull. A twenty minute walk from the farm. Change at Sandhills and take another train on to Waterloo Station. Then bus it to the College. A right drag! I wouldn't get back home till about 5~30pm! A long day, then home-work! Eventually my parents bought me a bike and I used to cycle to Crosby each day. It would take me, say an hour. Good early practise, Helen for reaching sixty plus would you not agree!!

I did not take advantage of the educational chance given to me. Nor did I like school any better now than I did in my earlier days. I learned a little of everything but a lot about nothing!! I played cricket for the College but could not play Rugby at College level because of the weakness in my left wrist due to the break I had sustained in the car accident years before. I did win the Half Mile Championship in the sports events held at The Hightown Rugby Club. For this I received a clock. Again, over the years it has disappeared. It was soon very noticeable that things were not right on the poultry farm. Hens were not laying. Some were dying and, most important, money was been lost and lost fast! Nothing seemed to be going right! It was indeed a period of great concern and worry for my Dad in particular.

In the end my Dad had to put everything up for sale. The farm house we did not own. It was rented, as was the grounds. It appeared the land had, for far too long, harboured fowl and therefore had become more and more unsuitable each year. So much for the friend of my Father who recommended and sold the place to him. All was eventually auctioned at a great loss of cash, with many items sold far below the listed price! Yet another stage of life had ended with the money all but gone and we had to move home once again.

I, at this stage, would be around twelve or so. Eileen, who was educated at a Convent in the Birmingham area had ,by now, finished her schooling. Our Uncle Jack in Ireland, paid for the education of both Eileen and cousin Marie. That was a policy of his. Giving the girls a good grounding.

We then moved to Earls Close in Crosby. A rented house off Warwick Avenue. My Mum was then pregnant with my brother, Jack and The Depression of the 1930's was just taking hold. Hence, my Dad had no job and no prospects for employment and no chance of returning to sea. I recall now how hard he tried for employment, but without any luck. He received no benefits whatsoever, for in those days anyone earning above a certain amount was barred from contributing weekly towards unemployment stamps while employed. Hence, no income at all! I remember my Dad taking on the selling of "Key Ring Insurance" on a commission basis. He would go from door to door, in all areas and all weathers and believe me, he made little or nothing each day. Certainly not enough to keep a family. The rent of the house where we lived was very high and what with my mother's confinement payments, money was indeed short and don't forget, my Father was still paying for my education at St Mary's College.

My Brother, Jack, was born in a Nursing Home in Norma

Road, Waterloo, on 13th April 1933. A dull place to say the least! I recall going there to visit my mum and thinking; "What a depressing place!" It certainly was bad luck that she should have to start once more, with a family after more or less getting us off her hands. She was 43 then and should have been relaxing with plenty of free time. Instead, here she was starting all over again! It must have been most difficult for her and it proved just that later on. Never did my Mum complain. Never did she fail to bestow all her love to our Jack and protect him from the many pit falls that he seemed to get into.

It was shortly after the birth of our Jack that my Dad decided it would be wiser to purchase a new house which had just being built. A smaller house, it was situated in Vermont Avenue, Crosby. The down payment was low and the repayments lower than where we were living. So again we moved home. My Mum and Dad had thirteen different homes during their marriage, Helen! Unfortunately Vermont Avenue was the last that they shared together.

Now, before I go on Helen I must relate another item about our doggie pal, Pete. It was when we lived in Allerton. Eileen used to dress him up in baby clothes. Put a bonnet on him and place him in her doll's pram, pushing him all around the place. He would lay with his head on the pillow enjoying every minute of it! One day as Eileen pushed him along another dog started to bark at the pram, so Peter took off, dashing after this dog and, of course, with having the baby clothes on, kept falling and rolling in the gutter. In the end, exhausted and looking fed up because he could not catch the other dog, he just gave up. The baby clothes were all torn and sister Eileen was not amused. When we moved to the poultry farm Peter came and we had more problems for there was a watch dog there called Prince. Well, he was real jealous of Peter running free and would go mad every time Peter ventured out. Now Peter knew just how far Prince's chain would stretch and he would sneak along the hedge and when near Prince, dash off with delight knowing that the other dog could not reach him! Yes, you've guessed it. One day he became too cocky and Prince caught him and, of course, a big fight ensued. We tried to stop them when Prince's tooth got stuck in the name plate of Peter's collar. Peter was becoming unconscious so, at this point, my Dad picked up a White-Wash Brush and belted Prince over the head. Knocking him out and ending the fight with both dogs laying flat out on the ground.

Despite this aggressive side to him, Prince was a very

affectionate dog. He loved to be made a fuss of. He had always been a guard dog and used to do his block when ever the men arrived with the meal etc! when we sold up he too was sold. He was a wire-haired terrier, where as Peter was a smooth-haired terrier. Peter came with us to Earls Close and then to Vermont Avenue. He used to go out on his own, roaming around Crosby at leisure. But one day he was knocked down by a car on Liverpool Road and brought home by a neighbour who knew him. He was taken to the Vet and because he had internal injuries he became rather cross and could hardly move. We had to decide what was best for the poor dog and agreed it was better to have him put down. A sad sad day for me !

So endth a long and happy friendship with a real pal and a sad, sad time to say the least.

It was shortly after we lost Peter that my Mum heard of a family whose dog had just had pups and knowing we had lost a pal, suggested we have one of them. Dad was asked and he said yes. So again we started with a pet who turned out to be great.

## Chapter 3
# Early Working Life

It was while I was on school holiday shortly after we had moved that I heard of a job going at the Co-Operative Milk Depot in Moor Lane, Crosby. What with thinking of the situation concerning the finances of the family, and also, I must admit, my lack of interest in the College, I decided to try for the job. I was successful!

I went home to spring the surprise. Obviously there was trouble as they, my parents, wanted me to have a good education and possibly a good job. In the end they appreciated my willingness to help with the income and after much deliberation they consented.

So my life of employment had begun. I was then just turned fourteen years of age and my job consisted of pulling a hand-cart around filled with milk bottles. Delivering in the area of Liverpool Road, Myers Road East and all roads off there. Not a great job for an ex college pupil, but I felt free and independent with no worries of studies, homework etc. Peace at last!

I used to start at 7 AM. Finish about 11-30am. Restart at 1-30pm and finish after the later round which was about 3 PM. The second round I did on my bike so it didn't take long. I did this job for quite some time, getting many soakings and plenty of muscles. I enjoyed the work but unfortunately, one morning while pulling out of the shop, six crates, each containing two dozen bottles crashed to the ground. The lower crate, which was broken, caused the lot to fall. In all about two/three dozen full bottles of milk were smashed. Now this type of accident had happened previously to another member of the staff and it had been accepted as unavoidable. But, this time the firm said I had to pay for the breakages. This I refused to do as I considered mine an accident also! The firm sent out an Inspector to plead with me to change my mind, promising that I could make progress in the job, but on principle I would not alter my decision. So, a couple of weeks later I was finished up. Many friends I made during that period. Nibby Rudd, who also worked at the Co-Op and lived in Alexander Road. We used to check on each other for getting up in time for work.

In the house in Vermont Ave. I slept in a small room off the Kitchen and it was handy for such occasions. Also for when I would come in late. Eric Hitchcock, who lived next door and his cousin Stan Field were mates also. George Martin, Norman Evans, George Holmes. Just to name but a few. Parties were numerous. Fun was foremost and teenage life was taking shape.

My Dad was successful in obtaining a post with the Mercantile Seamans' Association as a Representative. It was the Union for Ships Masters and Mates.

My sister also was working. I think at this time she was training to be a Nurse. She did a spell at the Hanaman Hospital in Hope Street then over to Chester Royal. In the end she gave it all up. I remember a lot of trouble at home because she would not continue in that profession, but as it all effected her nerves she had to leave.

I had taken a job in Hall's Furnishers Store in South Road. That was only temporary as I was awaiting a start in a small garage in Sandheys Ave. This was a one man (plus two of us apprentices) firm and was most interesting.

As time went on my Dad arranged for me to go to sit the Pilot Service Exam and Tests at the Custom-House, Pier Head. If passed I would have entered into training to skipper the Pilot tugs as they guided the huge ocean going liners into the docks. I recall six or seven candidates sitting, but none of us obtained a full pass mark and were turned down.

Now it so happened Helen, a cousin of mine, around that period did get through and unfortunately some three/four years later lost his life when the Pilot Boat sank in a heavy storm in the Mersey. All Hands were lost as the incident happened in the early hours of the morning and when it became daylight the ship had,at the time of the disaster, been quite near to the coast, close to Formby. But all communication was completely lost and the crew did not know where they were as the steering gear had snapped and they were just drifting around. Who knows! Was that an omen or was my time not due?

I next decided I would try for The Royal Air Force as a pal of mine from Maghull, who also went to Saint Mary's College and who I always kept in touch with, was applying. Mind you, we had spoken about this previously and it was because I had it in mind when I had the trouble with the Co-Op that gave me that extra couldn't care less attitude. I didn't, in fact, think it would take so long, but at last, here I was with high hopes of new horizons as I awaited a reply. I was accepted and duly went to West Drayton for exams and Medical. The Exams I passed OK but the medical was my downfall!

You see Helen, they could be choosy at that time and a possible new entrant had to have a full complement of teeth. Well, at that time, I had two or three missing. Everything else went good, but alas it was not to be! I came home a very disappointed young lad and found myself out of work. My pal did, in fact, pass and was accepted as a Photographer! Wonder what ever happened to him?

My term of unemployment did not last long for I got a job at Gardners Printing Works in Hawthorne Road, Litherland, starting on night work folding Vernons Football Coupons by machine. To this day I can still taste the Bacon and Egg butties that my sister used to make for me to take to work. Eileen was then working at Vernons Pools in Aintree.

The night work was usually only for a couple of nights at a time. Mainly Sunday night and Monday night. Then it would be back to day-time working. I used to cycle to work and while on days used to meet up with Madge on her bike going to Lewis Clothing Factory, also in Litherland.

Reckon I fancied her even then as every Saturday and Sunday all Boys and Girls used to meet up and walk down South Road Waterloo. It was known as "The Bunny-Run"! One would move up and along that road numerous times per visit. At the shore end there would usually be representatives of the emerging fascist political movements, The Black-Shirt Mob or the Green-Shirt Mob with their respective heavy gang surrounding them. Their leaders would be shouting out their policies and trying to recruit new members. We were not interested in that sort of thing, but enjoyed watching the many fights that broke out between those mobs and the older chaps that stood and argued with them. Police patrolled the whole road and kept moving everyone on, although the police held no jurisdiction on any political debates that gathered in numbers on the shoreline. Hence the two Mobs which, incidentally were better avoided, were never moved on.

Boys and girls would meet, make dates etc. Perhaps go into a small shop which sold Pop and sit down until the Owner would chase you out if he thought you had been loitering too long. Bridge Road, Litherland was another such Bunny~Run and we would occasionally go there for a change of faces. I used to meet Madge inside The Queens Picture House in South Road on an odd Saturday. She never had enough money to pay for me as well. It cost six pence( about 21p in today's money)That was a lot of money in those distant days! We sometimes went to the Winter Gardens cinema in Church Road, Waterloo. They mostly had scarry thrillers on, but the Queens was the favourite!

I recall on a number of Saturday nights at the Pics I would get cramp at the top of my leg from playing football. It affected me often as I played regularly.

Gardners had a team in The Shipping League and I was one of the eleven players. While I am on about the Queens Picture House I must tell you that Madge worked there part time for a spell and while she did a few of us used to get in for nothing! Great!

Now Helen, where was I?

Oh yes! The Gardners Football Team were very successful and one year we won The Lever Cup. We played the final on the Cheshire Lines Ground in Allerton where I used to go and watch the football when I was little and when we lived there. Strange that!

While working at Gardners I was put into the Ruling Department and after a short spell was capable of setting up and looking after a couple of machines. It was whilst I was at Gardners that a number of the chaps decided to go along with another lad and join the Territorial Army in Tramway Road, Aigburth. I asked my next door neighbour pal, Eric and his cousin, Stan, if they also wanted to join?

We all went up and enlisted.

That was in 1938.

The Unit was called the Lancashire Fortress, Royal Engineers. We used to cycle up to Aigburth for drills and cycle back home again. Sometimes twice a week. If the weather was bad we would bus it! We used to get expenses which was quite handy and, of course, our Bounty money as well which, at that time, was £5.

Weekend Camps spent at Altcar Rifle Range learning to fire properly or weekends at Crosby or Perch Rock Batteries were great and we enjoyed them very much.

Annual Camps in Northern Ireland and Tynemouth were something special. Even in those days one had to be careful in Northern Ireland for political sectarian trouble was there then although on a much lighter scale, such as tarring and feathering a person who belonged to a different religion. Or tying them to a lamp-post! One had to be very careful of one's Rifle as it could go missing, at the drop of a hat and be used for terrorist purposes.

I concentrated on the engineering side of the Unit. Running and maintaining the powerful engines which generated the power for the search lights which scanned the river for any hostile vessels. Not that there were any around at that period. We all had our special section. Some on search lights. Others on controlling the lights, and, of course, Engine Room Staff. Our camps were like a holiday as we used to be free most evenings except when there was an exercise with the Artillery firing at targets out at sea. Those camps were great! We enjoyed them and ,of course, there was the coming home! Now that was special indeed. Everyone welcoming you and most of all the Bunny-Run Girls! One felt like a hero! Happy days!

Now I forgot to mention, Helen, that in September 1937 Eileen had her 21st Birthday Party. It was held at Fletcher's Dancing School in Oxford Road, Waterloo. She was a member there and we all had a great time. Many friends turned up and I recall there was plenty of fun and laughter that night. I don't recall just what presents she got but the party itself was a gift! I was 18 at the time, growing up and enjoying life. Always out. Always with mates and enjoying the special entertainment that was put on around the Borough, like bands in the parks, Both dance and military concerts were occasions when everyone knew where to find one's friends.

When I was 19 years of age, in 1938, there was a crisis with Germany and we were called up. I remember, at the time, Eileen being home on her own when the Police arrived. Mum and Dad had gone to the theatre in Liverpool and Eileen was babysitting.

I was out and when I did arrive home here she was cleaning my uniform buttons. Poor Eileen! Eric too had been out and arrived home about the same time. We threw on our kit and took most of our stuff with us! Dashing off for the bus to take us to Tramway Road. My Mum and Dad had come home and everyone expected this was the end of the world! Tears were many before we parted. But to us young lads it was excitement! Something different! And as we did not know just what to expect the mystery remained within us.

On reaching Tramway Road we were bedded down till the next morning. Some of the lads who lived near were allowed to go home once they had booked in. As for us, we lived too far away so stayed. The next morning, bright and early, we were split up into three groups. One going to Barrow-In-Furness. One to Perch-Rock Battery ,New Brighton. I was included in the Crosby Battery Group. We were on alert for about four or five days and on the Saturday or Sunday evening they said we could all go home as War had been averted!! We were instructed to return to our depot on the following Monday for further instructions.

I recall at that time, the then Prime Minister, Neville Chamberlain ,waving a piece of paper in the air and saying. "This states that our two great nations; Germany and Great Britain will never go to war again!" Well, lets be honest, all that did was to give this country time to get a little stronger and more prepared than it was! Anyway, needless to say we were all overjoyed at being set free, so to speak and dashed along the shore to South Road to meet up with the lads and lassies once again.

The weather during those years was very dependable. The summers were beautiful and every Sunday we would all meet down on the shore. Pitch a tent, play rounders, swim and always plenty of laughter and fun. We would stay there till half five to six, then home, tea, change and off to The Bunny Run, showing off our sun-burn, which, at times did hurt a lot, for we had no sun tan lotion and we would peel a lot until, after a few days, the brown tan took over. Then all was O.K!

I remember Eric's mother putting Bicarb with water on our backs and it used to be freezing cold, but it helped I think. My girl friend at that time was Joan Godfrey. A cousin of George Martin and, as Eric was courting her mate we often made up a foursome. We all were appreciating our young lives and although we never traveled far in those days, the routine was acceptable. All was going so good. Family life with baby Jack at an interesting stage. Everyone working and always so much to do. It seemed perfect!

On occasions Eileen and I would go to the pictures. We were still good friends. The close relationship that we had when growing up remained and I don't honestly remember us ever falling out! I would kid her along when we would queue up for the picture show by saying don't get too close! People will think you are my girl friend! Yes, I think everyone was enjoying themselves in one way or another.

But, lo and behold, late 1939 changed all that for again the troubled world brought more conflict between nations.

## Chapter 4
# Called Up For Service
# And War

So it was, in August of that year, we, as Territorials, were again called up for service. The routine was as before except this time I was posted to the Perch Rock Battery. Stan Field and Johnny Smith were in our section and so we knocked about together when off duty. Funny thing with Johnny Smith. We had gone to school together and when I went to work in Gardners, he was working there as well and when we joined the T A. he too joined. Now here we were again!

Our first working session in New Brighton saw us digging a very large, long, air raid shelter in the park adjacent to the promenade. We were on duty every night at the Battery and slept during the day. Our billets were The Empress Ballroom in the main street on Victoria Road. Very roomy! We had one section and the Artillery the other. We were granted leave each second or third week for a few days. This was when we had got into a working routine. I would come home to see my Mum and Dad and take Joan out. When I was unable to come home Joan would come over to New Brighton on a Sunday and we'd spend a few hours together.

We remained as a Unit for some months and were enjoying the Army life, close to home, reasonable duties, plenty of time to have a drink for when on late shift we did not go on duty till eleven o'clock or before the tide was due in. This was because the sea water would cover the Slip Way and once that happened you could neither get into or out of the Battery until the tide went out again. We did, on one occasion, hang back pretending to be doing something with the result that when we got to the Slip Way we couldn't get through! The Corporal in charge was put on a charge for his crew had to stay for a further few hours! We never got away with that move again!

We had formed a Football team and played a number of

games using the then called Brighton Football Ground which was very good indeed. Eileen was living over in New Brighton at that time, staying with a pal of hers. She had had a row at home with Dad and moved out! It was good for me as I could go round and see her any evening. All at that period was going fine but alas big changes were coming up for it was decided to disband the Lancashire Fortress so allowing the Artillery to take over the whole duties of the three Batteries and allowing us Royal Engineers to be freed for other commitments. Permission was given for anyone wishing to remain could do so! With the Artillery instructing them in our work. John Smith did just that and I was surprised for to remain with the Artillery was like a Liverpudlian football fan becoming an Everton football supporter!

But John was an Evertonian, so what could you expect? I must be honest and say that since I have met John again, he says that he, like the others, was detailed and directed to remain. So I reckon he must be right! But I sure missed him for he, Stan and I were real good pals! Eric, by the way, had gone to Barrow-In-Furness, and, of course we did not see him. The move also meant that I could not see Eileen and when we heard we were moving to the east coast, Scarborough, it seemed like the other side of the world!

The rest of the unit joined up together and we set out, after Dunkirk to form the 580th Army Troop Engineers Company. Our duties were concentrated on defences along the East Coast of England. We had a lot of new recruits from all over the country. Also, a number of lads from Ireland who had volunteered.

Our Territorial Army experience was used to train these chaps and eventually the Company passed out as a qualified Unit. We spent a short period as bomb disposal as the German Air Force was bombing all along that area and we were clearing sites looking for victims unfortunate enough to loose their lives at this early stage of the conflict. It was so sad to come across bodies with people crowding around to see if it was a relative or friend.

We then moved to a place called Histon in Cambridge. A small spot where we were split up into different billets. Stan was transfered to another section. Eric too was in another section so I paled up with a chap named Johnny Marsh. It was while we were in this village and I was home on leave that, instead of returning at the end of my granted period, I overstayed a couple of days! There were about four of us who overstayed and, of course we were put on a charge. We got 14 days C.B. Each morning we had to parade in full battle kit with everything highly polished and blancoed. In the middle of our sentence the unit again moved, still in Cambridge, but this time to a place called March. Each section was again in different billets and we were all doing further, up graded training with a view to going over seas. The N.C.O s were hard at work with all this extra training and what with our continued parades with full cleaned kit, we too were worn out! There were a few of us on jankers and we did manage to sneak out a couple of times when it was dark! Avoiding the known spots, we were nearly caught one night but managed to get back to the billet before the N.C.O! I remember ,Helen, that although I was on jankers I was allowed to go and play football for the unit for although I was not captain . I, with a Sargent, who trained us would choose the team to play. The football captain was a Sargent so, by army ethics, that position was his. I was considered a fairly decent player. We played local teams and included in our season was a couple of games against West Ham whose complete team were serving as an Anti-Air-Raid-Unit. I recall we lost one and drew the other. I, along with two other members of our team, were asked to be guest players for the local team of March. A similar team to Marine, an amateur local football club. Permission had to be sort from our C.O. first and, as I had completed my jankers all was well. As a matter of fact, as soon as I'd finished my C.B. I was put on a Cadre Class and ended up as a Lance-Corporal in my section, helping to further the training of the lads. My promotion was indeed a surprise to say the least especially just after doing fourteen days on a report! Guess it really was on merit! At least that's my tale!

My pal Eric was then a Drill Corporal in another section of our unit and very smart as well. The people of March were very nice and a chap named Mick Halksworth and I were invited to a house for odd meals etc. They treated us great and we used to come and go just like one of the family. Their name was Smith and I have among my photos one of them.

On one of my trips home for leave Joan and I got engaged. This was frowned upon by my parents as views were very strong in those days especially about religion and Joan was a non-Catholic! Still she was accepted and our families got on quite well.

Back at our army base, it was not long before we had

orders to move out for foreign parts. We said good bye to all our friends and marched to the station where we boarded a troop train and headed for Greenock in Scotland. They didn't, of course, tell us but that's where we arrived! There we boarded the Troop Ship "The Cape-Town-Castle". It was then late 1940. The year of my 21st birthday which I celebrated while in Scarborough. Call it celebrated only because that is the term used. I was on duty that day and, apart from cards, I received a parcel from home mainly consisting of food stuff etc. When I look back, Helen, over the years, I feel very bitter that our youth should have been denied to us. They say that the early twenties are years to remember, years to enjoy, years to spend sort of growing up and sharing the new found freedom of life. We lost all that. We lost all those years! We lost a section of our growing up and it could never be replaced. I, like many of my pals, went off at age 20 and came back age 26. Picking up the pieces but never regaining what we had lost. I suppose some will say we were lucky. We did come back! Others did not! That may be true! I lost many dear friends and pals and have vivid memories of each and everyone of them and their sufferings. No one wins in War! Everybody loses somewhere along the line!

We set sail for an unknown destination! We were in convoy and life aboard was mostly spent in leisure; swimming, deck games, playing cards and nightly bingo, With the wide boys running that! Our daily life boat drill used to go on for an hour or so and, of course, physical training for a further hour. Then relax!

Our first port of call was Gibraltar. We did not disembark but did lose one of our Officers who was taken ashore because of illness. We picked up more troops and, once more, back on the High Seas! We picked up another convoy and sailed on to South Africa. Cape Town was our port of destination, after a brief visit to Sierra Leone, where the locals would dive off their small boats for a Liverpool sixpence or Glasgow shilling as they called them. Lads tried wrapping half pennies in silver paper and throwing them into the water, but the natives could tell by the speed which the coin sank whether or not it was a coin of value worth diving for! We would buy fruit from them by lowering a basket over the side and they would put your request in and when you had hauled it up you'd return the money asked. It was all quite a marvelous sight!

Cape Town was a really lovely place and the vista upon approach was something to be seen to be believed with Table

Mountain most prominent and, of course, the sunshine on the water makes everything look beautiful. All countries in that part of the world have that advantage. We spent four fab days there being picked up by local people with cars and shown around places of interest including Table Mountain itself. After exploring these places they would take us back to their homes for a slap up meal. Returning to the ship about midnight.

The previous ships coming from Australia and New Zealand, en route to England, had caused no end of trouble and damage to the City. Hence the reason we were escorted on our trips ashore! I recall stories being told of those Anzacs and the way they carried on during their visit.
Stories such as chasing the beer carts, driven by Blacks and when the troops were catching up the Blacks would take off leaving the beer for the lads to sup. And they did! The lot! They'd go into Woolworths store, start dancing with the female staff, and, as soon as the Manager complained, they'd roll him up in a roll of lino and stand him up against the wall, then carry on dancing!

Another story concerned a pub they used to frequent. The pub manager, in an attempt to avoid too much hassle, told them they could do whatever they wished as long as they did not damage the clock on the wall as it was a family heirloom! They did, in fact ,wreck the pub. Also they continually called out the Fire Brigade to the bar. The Fire-Chief co operated with them to a point! So, when the time came for them to leave, the pub Manager discovered that his clock was missing! It appears they had taken it and presented it to the Fire Chief as a gift! Each and everyone of those men were fined to help pay for the damage they had caused and the fines went on for years!

What impressed me most about that country was the bunches and bunches of grapes hanging over the front doors of the houses! It was the first time that I had seen such things in such abundance and naturally they stuck in my mind!

Fruit itself was really cheap! We went to the market one day and brought loads back to the ship for only coppers! After the four days were up we set sail and continued to enjoy the journey through the Red Sea and so on. As we guessed, towards Egypt!

We were fortunate on the voyage for we were billeted in cabins. Four berth! Most of the troops were bedded down in the dance halls etc. So our lot was more comfortable and more relaxing! Guess it was because we came from Liverpool, or, at least, a few of us did and we deserved the best!

Eventually, after eight weeks on the High Seas, we arrived at Port Taufiq at the end of the Suez Canal. Never out of England before! Age 21 and all at once, thousands of miles traveled! New adventures! New places! New faces! New ways of life! All suddenly happening! Without realising it, ones life was changing!

No longer the quiet, come day, go day approach! The slow, happy days shared with the ones you needed. The familiar faces. The love and affection that you had grown to accept as part of life.

The desire, even then, to return to a normal pattern of life was slowly but surely becoming less and less of a possibility! Our thoughts were "What is to come? Where am I going? What is happening to me?"

How confusing it all was and how little you could do about it! Your life was no longer your own. You did as others told you to do! You went where others told you to go and you followed the flow of a man's destiny for what ever the future held!.

Our journey out had been uneventful. Plenty of alerts, hence the boat drills just in case. On disembarking we were transported about ten miles outside Alexandria under canvas. I recall the days were very, very hot and nights really cold! We used to be plagued with scorpions and mosquitoes! Hence we didn't think much of that country! It used to be called the country of the Wogs and the Dogs, but it was pointed out to us that the word W-O-G which had branded the Egyptians from The First World War did in fact mean, Worthy Oriental Gentlemen. I can assure you Helen, that description was way out of character! They would rob you at any opportunity at all, as we found out to our cost on our first day there.

You see, we gave an Arab the money for fruit before we got the goods, so he took off and as we were on the train and it was going dark we could do nothing about it! But we did learn a valuable lesson!

We used to dash off to Alexandria, although it was out of bounds to our unit! It was a weird place and one had to be on one's guard all the time!

Flies were another curse. The locals would just sit there and let the flies crawl all over them while they'd sit about in the shade whereas we'd be swatting them off every few seconds! It was not long before we realised that a move was imminent for all the equipment that we brought over from Blighty, which was brand-new, was exchanged for old worn out desert kit including our vehicles as well. We packed up all our personnel kit and moved away from our camp reaching the harbour and boarding yet another ship.

This time it was "The Cameronian". We set sail for Greece with literally a load of rubbish as our weapons and defences! No other words could describe it!

That trip was quite eventful with dive bombers and fighter planes doing their best to sink us en route! We survived and landed at Piraeus Harbour to experience, yet another change to our lives!

*Chapter 5*
# Greek Campaign.

The weather in Greece was really beautiful. We were again under canvas in a deep, woody area and just below the Acropolis. What a wonderful sight that all is. History galore. We visited Athens, where to our dismay, German Soldiers were on duty outside their Embassy as they were not at that time at war with Greece. It was most disturbing, to say the least and we had been warned to keep away from that area as after a few drinks anything could have happened. It was not long before they declared war on the Greeks. The Italians in Albania, which bordered Northern Greece, were getting a real hammering by the Albanians and Greeks, and the Hun, seeing all the British Troops coming in, knew that we would walk through "The Wops" the way things were, so it was to help their partners in crime that they made their decision.

As we expected we were soon on the move North, through small villages with broken-down shacks as homes. Goats, hens, and even pigs living under the same roof. People, very friendly but so poor. It was unbelievable! (another new to us all) The mountainous passes were so narrow, with a sheer drop down one side and were only wide enough in places for a truck so if we'd meet Greeks with donkey carts coming the other way, we simply had to tip the cart, less donkey, over the side as blocked roads only held up the convoy. We would pass many Italian prisoners who had been marched South by one or two Greek guards. The figure would be simply hundreds upon hundreds and it amazed us to see so many in one group. Mind you Wops were not worth a light anyway.

On we went until reaching Mount Olympus, a large plain where the Olympic Games first took place. This was to be our base and we would be transported further North to carry out our duties. As the advance of the Italians with the German troops help was pretty rapid since they officially declared war on Greece, and as they bombed the only Bridge over the northern river (the name I can not remember), our unit had to hurriedly erect a Bridge for the fast retreating British, Australian, New-Zealand and Greeks who could not hold the might of an army with full control of the air. That river was completely red with the blood of fallen troops and upon completion the bridge was in full use and I'll bet it did not last long. We withdrew fast from the immediate area and I well remember the Aussies whom we were attached had forward canteens, very much forward believe me. They sold bottles of whiskey for almost nothing and as if it was going out of fashion. To say the ANZAC'S were always pissed would be correct and because of this they would mount a Machine-Gun on a high point and while awaiting Hun troops, whom advanced in trucks and would alight a short distance away, they, the Aussies, would open a betting stake as to how many Huns they would knock out with Machine-Gun fire. This meant they would be firing up to the last minute thus allowing the retreating troops more time to withdraw. They would then pick up their winnings and fly off. Wonder how many of them enjoyed the extra cash.

It became more and more difficult to hold up the advance as the German planes would fly just feet from the ground, Machine Gunning at will. There were NO British Planes at all in Greece and it became more and more clear that all those troops sent to Greece were merely being used as a Stop-Gap for spreading the enemy out as far as possible, also possibly as a token gesture to the Greek Government. We were daily dive bombed and strafed many times in a day and some of my pals were killed in this way. One being Stan Field who had shared my peace time life as one of the crowd. He was also Eric Hitchcock's cousin. He was killed instantly when returning in a truck from carrying out a duty up the line, He was buried more or less where he fell. This spot I cannot recall but I have often thought of paying a visit to his burial ground and paying my respects to a friend and pal. Don't suppose I will, but who knows! I know I would need to contact the Army Cemetery Organisation and see what information they could give me. Stan was a bricklayer by trade, serving his time with Costains. He loved to play cards and would gamble on anything. He enjoyed Guinness as a drink, always full of fun and loved life. We would go to the football at Anfield on a Saturday then back to his house for tea. He lived off Merton Road near to the Flyover. His family were very nice and I spent many happy hours there. Memories!

The weather up in the North of Greece was terribly cold with snow storms quite heavy. This, after hot sun shine and high temperatures in Athens, didn't help at all. Our trip down Greece was a night-mare. Continually under fire. No rest. No sleep. Absolutely exhausted! I do recall at one point when, due to torrential rain and sleet there was a lull and many of us just threw our ground-sheets down where we were, putting our Gas-Capes over us and falling asleep despite the terrible weather. Unfortunately the rain etc. stopped and the nightmare started again. One of my section, a lad from Birmingham said "I'll stay by you Frank, for if I'm going to die, I don't mind it happening with you!" My reaction was "Piss off Brumie! I'm not due to go yet!"

I recall that, at that moment, as I dived for cover I landed right in a load of dog dirt and that meant to me Good-Luck, even under those circumstances. Don't know what ever became of him.

Eventually after retracing our way down those narrow passes with many dead and wounded laying around. With bombed vehicles and their loads having to be moved to clear a way through, we reached Athens once again looking much the worse for wear. Battle worn and soaked to the skin. After a slight holdup we continued by truck to the harbour of Pireaus where we had arrived some weeks previous. The people of Greece, all looking sad and frightful of what the future would hold, stood on the pavements throughout the city, fearing the worst, yet managing a wave and a look of Thank-You-For-Trying.

We had not been at Pireaus Harbour long before the sirens sounded and we scattered in all directions looking for a safe hideaway. Fortunately no raid took place. It was an observer plane, planning, no doubt, what was to come. We were issued with food for the first time for so long we wondered if, perhaps we'd starve to death instead of ----. As we waited on the quayside watching the movement of many of the stretcher and walking wounded being brought to the area where one boat was tied up, we learned that the boat was in fact, King George of Greece's Yacht, called "The Hellas". All those wounded, stretcher and walking, were taken aboard as were civilians, including, women, young and old, also children. By now many more troops had arrived and, to our surprise, we were given the order to board ship. Fully expecting that this ship was indeed a Red-Cross-Ship, but NO, and after all, orders are orders, so on we marched. With so many getting on, there was little room to spare, so we went on the top deck having been issued with additional ammunition and instructed that if a raid took place, then concentrated rifle fire was very effective, as had been proved at Dunkirk.

The gang planks were pulled in and all was set for sail, but unfortunately, due to so many being on board, the boat was unable to float, it was aground! We were instructed to move over to Starboard side, in the hope that this would allow the boat to right itself and so sail away. But no. So it was decided that we would have to wait until the tide came in at about 7-30pm so allowing the boat to re float. In the mean time they sent a diver down to investigate for any damage. They were now issuing food on a lower deck and my mate, Johnny Marsh said he would go and collect some for him and I. He left me his ammo and rifle and away he went. I had earlier been to collect food as well so we'd be well stocked for a long trip to Egypt. Most of the troops had gone from the top deck. Only a few Greeks plus a handful of other troops including Lea Carter and myself remaining. It was then about 7pm, on Thursday the 24th April 1941.

As we talked and as we reminisced about the previous few weeks, we heard the now familiar drone of Hun planes approaching and looking skywards, sure enough we saw about seven heading in our direction. They started to dive and as they did we immediately made for the stairway, forgetting the instructions on concentrated rifle-fire, and wasn't it just as well, for as we reached the stairway, a couple of Greek's stopped to look, I pushed them down, falling on to my back as I did. The planes were machine gunning as they approached and bullet holes were appearing all along the deck, some just missing my head by inches. By the law of averages, had we remained on that deck firing, we would most certainly have been no more.

By the time I was on the lower deck I could see everyone laying down awaiting the next and more important matter. That of bomb dropping! I joined them and a couple of Aussies also shared that deck spot with me. The first bomb to fall hit me for my watch stopped at eight minutes pass seven. I could then feel all sorts of things falling down upon me. I felt smothered. Every blow brought pain but I dare not move. I learned later that five bombs in all, struck the boat. One falling down the funnel and blowing out the engine room.

It was, I guess, about fifteen or so minutes after the commencement that people started to move. I had visions of being trapped as so much debris was on top of me. I had to, not only push all that off, but also the two Aussies that I shared that part of the deck with. They both appeared dead to me for they made no effort to move at all. As I moved I saw the whole ship in flames. The heat was terrific and I received burns, not only from the fire but also from the boiling water that was spraying down from the steam-pipes from the bombed boilers. The smoke made it pretty dark and I could not at that stage see the state of my arm, thinking it was just possibly broke I carried it to my chest making my way off that HELL-AS.

The sights that I saw while making for land still linger in my memory and will I'm sure forever. I saw a poor women with both her legs trapped and flames all around her shouting out for help. Little I could do, or anyone else for that matter, for she disappeared with the complete section of the deck. Ammunition was shooting off all over the place. Boxes having been loaded at the same time as we boarded, it was going off in all directions and making things more difficult. The screams of women and children and men still alive was terrible. The panic to get off was in full plight and as I went over threadbare decks I saw hundreds of soldiers and civilians laying dead below. I saw a girl pinned to a cabin door with shrapnel through her stomach. Bits of arms, legs, heads and bodies lay all over the place. Blood was pouring from everywhere. What terrible sights! What horrific scenes! These needed to be seen to be believed. It's not easy to just read and visualise. One has to be there at the time to realise how such tragedy becomes imprinted in one's mind, never to be forgotten.

I eventually found the gang plank which had been replaced. Many soldiers and civilians had dived and been blown, overboard. A lot drowned due to the oil on the water from the vessel. Those that managed, popped up covered in oil and, looking for assistance out of the tide. Among them the diver who had gone down earlier. By now I was in the daylight and looked at my arm. What a shock! I could see the shattered bone running down, with flesh hanging down and blood pouring from it. The pain was dreadful! I didn't know whether to laugh, cry, shout or what. My whole uniform was red with blood! My boots also were red and my feet soaked. Not all my blood I'm sure, but I must have looked a terrible sight. To make matters worse there were Fifth Columnists firing from the warehouse roof tops at those alighting from the stricken ship. There were some troops laying on the ground, most lightly the results of those bastards!

I staggered across the dock coming to a high wall which I was unable to negotiate, but recall just laying back and rolling over, picking myself up somehow and heading for the cover of a warehouse. There I saw one of our Staff-Sergeants who didn't help really as he immediately said "God! What a mess that arm is."

He did put a shell dressing on and as I could not keep still, although feeling very weak, I didn't even thank him for the little he did for me which at least stopped me looking at it and feeling sorry for myself. I moved on and then a chap took my watch off, which as I said had stopped at eight minutes past seven. An Aussie put a further bandage around my wrist and took me to an Air-Raid shelter where someone gave me a shot of whiskey. Blokes were laying all over the place, wounded something awful. Mine was mild compared to some of them but to me, bad enough.

A Greek came and took me outside where I saw Johnny Marsh looking OK but never spoke to him. Another of our unit, Frank Wardrope, asked if I'd seen Mick Halksworth, but I hadn't. Confusion and concern was in everyone's mind. I heard there was a direct hit on the Cabins where the stretcher cases were, killing them all. How many died on that ship I never knew. It must have been an awful lot. Many years later upon reading an extract from a book which contained a section on the evacuation of Greece it did say very few did survive the Hellas Bombing. I do know that our unit was disbanded due to the heavy losses in that campaign.

The Greek took me to an Ambulance which was full of lads shouting out with pain and terrible wounds, uncovered and bleeding profusely. The vehicle moved off, and outside the dock gates people stood crying, sharing the suffering of everyone. What they could see had upset them and many were praying, dropping to their knees showing much sympathy for us all.

Suddenly the Ambulance pulled up with a jerk! The driver had seen the people start to run and he too took off leaving us all at the mercy of a further raid. Fortunately, although planes were over head, no bombs dropped. They were most lightly heading further afield to cause more distress.

Another driver took over the wheel and we finished up at a Greek Hospital close to the town of Athens. This hospital was packed out with many, many casualties and some who had dived overboard and were there to rid themselves of oil etc. Among them was Eric Hitchcock. He was pleased to see me alive, and me to see him also alive. Sergent Millwater too had dived over and his reaction was to hug me and wish me good luck with my injuries, with a message to keep smiling. How hard that was under the circumstances and the scenes around! I heard later that both of them had saved many others from the water. Eric started to cut my jacket off while I waited in the endless queue to see the Doctors. The pain was killing me and after quite a long time I eventually went in to see a Greek Doctor. He could speak no English and of course me no Greek. He said something that sounded like, cut! I nearly went mad fearing amputation. I did the actions. He shook his head. I breathed again. As a matter of fact I recall, he did the action of boxing!

Courage was what I needed and the ability to fight my way through this. That gave me a little confidence, if no relief. I was taken by a civilian down below to an underground ward. There I had to wait as many in a worse condition were before me. I saw Bert Hutton on a stretcher. He had blood pouring from his mouth and throat. Poor Bert died later and he could have stayed in Blighty as a Drill Instructor at Chester Barracks, but wanted to be with us, his old colleagues. I can still see the look in his eyes as he focused on me passing his stretcher. He told me on the way out to Egypt not to mention to his wife the fact that he could have remained in England. How sad it all turned out for them both Helen. Just another chapter in the tragedies of war.

I was taken into another room to get fresh dressings as the blood had seeped through and in there was a girl screaming terribly. She had a piece out of her thigh the size of a dinner plate! The nurse was doing her best for all. They were worked to a stand still! My arm was put on a cage that was strapped to my body but that did not ease the pain one little bit. Gee! I prayed for something to be done to relieve the pain as it appeared to be getting worse. What with the arm and the burns on my face, life was a mess to say the least. They cut the rest of my blood soaked clothes off and put me into a ward bed. I couldn't rest or sleep despite being exhausted. Many were dying all around me! The shouts and moans were heartbreaking. Some of my unit colleagues were close to me. One, in particular, who spotted me kept shouting out "Frank. Please, please, help me.

Please get someone to do something for me. Help! I can not breathe properly."

Now the nurses and Doctors were so busy they couldn't attend to everybody who needed attention. This lad, Phil Barker, did eventually get rushed to the operating theatre.

At about three or four the following morning a number of us were moved out by Ambulance to a British temporary hospital at the Cecil Hotel in Athens. The trip was pure murder! Six of us on stretchers in the one vehicle, thrown around something awful! I think the driver had about four smashes en-route! He appeared to want to get rid of us as soon as possible for he must have been doing sixty mph all the way. Every bump brought shouts of pain from all inside. Not good drivers I can assure you!

A Major Fosbrook was in charge at that Hotel and if ever a man was entitled to a decoration for devotion to duty, it must have been him for he not only spent all day in the operating theatre but most of the night as well. He was on call at any moment to attend to the many patients who flooded into his small hospital. His efforts and dedication relieved much suffering in those dark days. He did a wonderful job and many must have to thank him for their condition and recovery, for I know that, correct, early treatment is so essential to an overall recovery. I was operated on the first night of arrival, and upon coming to the following morning, I saw a number of our company in different beds around the ward. Les Barnet died that day having had a few operations including a leg off, but he could not be saved.

As you can guess the 580th Army Troop Company was completely finished as a unit. We had lost so many lads in The Greek Campaign that it was impossible to form up again. Some of the less wounded left the hospital to try and get out of Greece, making their way south. The few English Nurses left on the Saturday and Greek Nurses took over. Then on Sunday 27th April 1941, I, with many of my colleagues were taken Prisoner-of-War while laying in our hospital beds. The Huns came into the wards, made us sign a form that we would not escape. (We couldn't anyway, as few of us could walk never mind escape!) They left guards on the outside of the hospital and then news came through that Athens had fallen. That, at the time, did not mean an awful lot to us as our minds were more on the medical problems that we had. The agony of every day. The thoughts of when will we be fit? When can we, once again, move about as before? Regain our full strength and cast off the shadow of being below A-one.

*Chapter 6*
# Prisoner Of War

So started my long, long sentence of imprisonment. Little did I know what the future held for me and it was just as well believe me.

On the Monday following the fall of Athens, they decided to remove the dressings from my arm, but as they got nearer the wound the dressing had stuck right inside and I could not bear the attempts to clear it so they stopped. This was after about an hour of probing. Gosh Helen, I suffered that lot beyond words! Those days were hell. Real hell! The pain was terrific. I could not sleep at night or in the day time either. I just smoked one after the other and longed for home and for loved ones. How!

When one is suffering and in so much agony one wants family, especially one's Mother. As a child, when you fell, receiving a cut or bang, the first thing was to run to your Mother. Her comfort, understanding and love made you feel that much better. You would stop crying without any treatment at all! Oh! How I wanted my Mum then is unbelievable! I needed her so much and I'm sure I could have got over my suffering much easier with her love. Her touch. Her understanding. Her smile to help and guide me through. But, alas, we were hundreds of miles apart and no chance of the needed love. The problem was mine and had to be borne alone. How many times in the years ahead did my heart cry out for my Mother's affection? Countless, I can assure you.

By the Monday evening my wound started to bleed, soaking the bandages that they continued to add until Major Fosbrook was brought in to the ward on the Tuesday morning with the bed now soaked in blood also. Panic stations were now the order of the day for I was passing out due to loss of blood. So, at once, without further delay I was rushed into the operating theatre suffering with a severe hemorrhage. I don't know how long I remained in there, but the following morning when I came too, I felt a lot better and slowly improved as each day went by.

Again, "The Hun" decided to move us all to another tem
porary hospital. Another nightmare ride! This time by "The
Hun" and I'm sure they did it on purpose knowing each
movement meant pain. The journey seemed to take hours when
in fact it was only probably a lot less. At this hospital my arm
was put in plaster and after a few weeks, they decided to change
it. It was full of puss and when removed, my arm itself was
terribly thin with blisters all over from infection. My nails had
stopped growing and the skin just peeled from my hand.
Another plaster cast was put on. By this time I began to feel
stronger. The burns on my face were healing up slowly and I
started to look more like my self again. Yet the days were long
and the nights even longer. Not so much now due to pain and
suffering but to the mind trying to sort out the position one was
in at this moment in time. Not free anymore, to roam as one
pleased. To go as one pleased. It was a challenging existence.
Only broken by a colleague interrupting your thoughts with a
remark "How much money have you left?"

We pooled our cash and got the Greek nurses to purchase
for us what ever they could, especially cigs! Things were scarce
and prices going up fast, hence our few bob did not go far.

As time went by food became more and more scarce. Cigs
were finished and any drinks of tea were minus sugar and milk.
Hardships were slowly coming to bear and it was not long
before we were again on the move, by Ambulance, this time
to the 5th Aussie Hospital housed in a very old three story
building. The Greek nurses that we left behind were very upset
to see us go, and us to leave them, for they had become close,
being the only females we came in contact with. They had
looked after us well and seen many of us improving with their
care. As we left they showered us with flowers and there were
many tears shed on both sides. Some of my pals were still with
me and I made many new mates. I and some of my walking pals
would go around and visit the lads of the unit who were still
bedridden. Some were still in great distress and some were
dying even then. Sad. So sad!

My plaster was again removed. The Aussie Doctor said he
would graft as soon as possible for the wound was too big to
heal on it's own, but it never happened as the Crete wounded
were now coming in and they, quite rightly, took priority. Their
battle scars were fresh and needed immediate treatment. I recall
a New Zealand lad who had one leg off from the hip. The other
leg off just above the knee. One arm off above the elbow and the

other just below the elbow. He was so cheerful it made one feel ashamed. Unfortunately or fortunately, he died from Pneumonia some weeks later.

Another English lad, I remember being brought in from Crete. He had seven bullets in the head and had laid in a trench for days before he was found. Maggots were falling from his nose and after a visit from the Doctor in charge, they decided he was too far gone to operate on, so he was left in the bed. His bed was opposite to mine. He was semi-conscious and would keep saying "Let me go home. My Mum will look after me."

Poor lad. I knew just what he was thinking in that damaged brain of his. Home and loved ones, just like I have said. He was left to die, but one day he kept shouting for an orderly to bring him a bottle. Well none came. So, in the end and in desperation he slowly pushed the covering sheet back, rolled to the edge of the bed and passed water onto the floor! Now, because of this action, and when the Doctors heard about it, they admitted that the patient wasn't as far gone as was first thought and he was immediately operated upon with most of the bullets removed. I don't know if that lad survived or not for I was moved before his next operation.

When you think of the state and suffering that human beings are forced into because Heads of Countries see fit to declare War upon each other. Making life and everything else become less important than the problem created. I have seen so much loss of life. So much suffering. So much pain. Bourne by many and suffered alone. So much deterioration of the mind and body. So much loss of one's youth and time from one's loved ones that I feel bitterness beyond words! I feel unable to express myself or even accept that time heals. It might, in cases where one is prepared to forget and push such scenes out of the mind, but honestly, I think those are few and far between. After all they were mates,pals, colleagues. How can you not remember!

One day while laying on my bed in the ward watching an orderly with a brush handle pushing black things on the ceiling, I asked what he was doing and he said "Killing Bugs!"

Well, that was my first introduction to such things. I had never seen them before and wondered why the beds were standing in jars of water, That remedy was alright when the bugs were on the floor, but on the ceiling was another problem. From that moment on bugs became another nightmare of my captive life. They haunted me where ever I went and it only needed one bug to be close to me or bite me and I would come out in big itchy lumps all over my body. I saw lads literally rip their plasters off arms or legs because bugs had got inside and were biting, causing severe damage to wounds and causing infection as well.

As the many, many wounded were still coming in from Crete, the hospital was very much overcrowded so the decision was made to transfer those who could walk to an old Greek Barracks some half mile or so from the hospital. I was in the second batch duly transported to this bug ridden dump. When the sun shone through the glassless windows on to the long wooden platform which we had to sleep upon, through the cracks in between the planks you could see just a mass of moving black hordes of bugs! God! What a way to live! I used to go to sleep at night with my trousers tucked inside my socks, shirt buttoned up to the neck, sleeves down and a terrible fear of what would probably happen during the night, for all those black hordes came out at night! Needless to say I got little sleep, if any at all! I too got bugs down my plaster.

I was pals then with a lad named Ray Peacock from Sunderland. He was a member of our unit and we had met up in the hospital and transfered here together. He had a bullet through his shoulder which completely paralysed his right arm, so between us, him with his left arm and me with my right, we used to help each other no end. We would wash our clothes, one holding, the other rubbing together. Our washing didn't look too bad, but we had to keep an eye on it as it dried other wise it may have disappeared! Ray had spent sometime in a different Greek Hospital than I and some nurses from there used to come along outside the wire and throw a little food and a few cigs, also figs, over to us. It helped as food was little enough at this time. They must have left themselves short to give us what they had.

The Doctor in charge of this dump was named Francis. He was hopeless! Couldn't remember a thing about anybody. My plaster was removed because of infection and I had a minor operation. From then on I had to attend the dressing centre daily.

We used to have to queue for hours for the once a day hot meal. The ration was poor and at the end of dishing out I've seen lads fighting to scrape out the big tubs for extra! All because of hunger. Those, like us, who could not take part because of our injuries, it was a case of make do with what you got.

Air Raids were regular. An ammo ship was blown up in the harbour. (Where were those planes when we needed them, I wonder!) Dock installations were a continual target, but it didn't help us any. Lads used to jump the wire to escape almost every day. Some were successful in getting away. Some were shot. Others recaptured.

One particular day when the guards were firing at some blokes making a break, we all advanced towards the gate, showing our disgust. "The Huns" turned their guns into the camp and started firing into the air just above us. Needless to say we all withdrew pretty fast.

Things were hard. Outlook bleak. No future. Just a dim reality of hopelessness.

I continued with Vaseline dressings, but the wound would not, could not, heal on its own and a graft was now completely out of the question under the ever increasing pressure on the hospital and the fact that sterilisation of theatre equipment was so much a problem that only the essential operations were being carried out.

An Aussie orderly, who had been a male nurse back home, suggested that, as the doctor didn't seem to have a clue, he thought if he put Elastoplast directly onto the wound it may draw a film over and stop the continual weeping. He left it for about four days at a time. The removals were murder! But, eventually, it did sort of start to heal over, but it drew my lower fingers up and no way could I straighten them. Of course, my wrist was very limited in movement and all in all the hand looked a freak claw!

I recall going before a Repatriation Board. They said my radial nerve had been severed, therefore I would be unable to regain full use of the limb ever! This upset me as I did not fancy returning home anything but almost 100% fit and certainly not a cripple! After much thought and discussion with myself, I decided to ask to see the Specialist. After a long wait of a few weeks I was summoned to appear before the committee and duly had a complete, full and thorough examination of my injuries. After long deliberation, during which there appeared some divided opinions, it was finally pointed out that, if the Radial Nerve had severed, my thumb would in fact be laying the other way and upon withdrawing my "Repat Sanction" they informed me that, after skin graft, I should be able to regain quite a fair amount of use back into the arm and hand. Encouraging news indeed! Ray, my pal, had passed for "Repat" and some twelve months or so later he went home on the first Repatriation of Prisoners-of-War from Germany. By that time the use had returned to his arm and he was OK. I recall that as the use started to come back into his arm I used to let him cut my hair and one time I let him shave me with an open razor! Never again! He cut me to pieces. When he did arrive home he was given a long leave and then drafted back into the army. I know this because he wrote to me a couple of times while I was still a P.O.W. I lost touch with him later on.

A chap from my unit, Sam Weller, came from the hospital. He told me that Eric had been taken prisoner at Corinth in the south of Greece. He had met up with his brother George and got this information. I was pleased that he was safe though surprised he'd met up with his brother for they were in different units. As my pal Ray had gone back to the hospital for further treatment, I became friendly with a Marine, Jim Colclough. He was also a good pal and friend. He had wounds to his foot. A big lad, over six foot tall. Came from Doncaster and was a Dental Mechanic. At least he was training when war broke out. During those months in that camp I contracted Sand-Fly-Fever, Dysentery and Scabies! It was no wonder. It was a dump and no place for treating sick people I can assure you! Escapes from the camp were many. In one night alone 36 Officers and 12 men made a mass break~out. The following day we that remained, had to endure rather a rough time! Not all those that jumped the wire got fully away. Some were recaptured, looking much the worse for their efforts, but that was the luck of the draw. It was mainly because escape was so easy that "The Hun" decided they would close the camp and transfer all POWs to a more secure place.

All of us, in those days, were always at risk for none had been registered as official POWs with the protection of "The Geneva Convention" or The Red Cross Headquarters, so anyone shot was just described as a "battle casualty!" The Greeks were very good and sympathetic towards us. They would take chances, throwing bread and cigarettes over the fence. They would help to hide any escapees and many times found themselves being beaten with a rifle butt or shot out of hand! Courage they had! Despite the fact they were a conquered nation.

So it was on the 20th August 1941 that we were taken to a ship in the harbour and banged down the hole. We were given bread to last two days. The ration was very small indeed! Not enough to feed a bird, let alone a growing lad! One poor chap fell down the hole due to weakness and was taken away in a right mess.

The boat hugged the coast in case of interception and the trip took four days. Two days longer than anticipated, with no extra food given! It meant we were absolutely starving! Bear in mind, none of us knew where we were being taken. The hole was in complete darkness and fresh air limited to one plank only being removed.

At long last the boat docked at the port of Salonika in Northern Greece. Soldiers stood along the quayside with fixed bayonets and, believe me, there was trouble for hunger can force one to react in an aggressive manner. Many were hurt, but all were paraded through the main streets almost unable to walk. There were about 400 of us in all and about half an hour later we arrived at this army camp. Not before a number had collapsed and were literally dragged along the route. My blood was boiling and I can assure you that my character was slowly but surely altering from being an easy going, happy carefree youth. I was now becoming a non-trusting, aggressive person, with hate building up inside me. I hated being subdued. I hated being treated below my status. I hated being under threat. I despised anyone with a rifle. I wanted to smash each and everyone of them. I decided I would learn enough German to show my feelings. Frustration is a terrible thing and the only consolation I had was that I was not alone in my dilemma for many were beginning to show their anger and during my sentence (for that is what it was) I always found Scotsmen the best of all. For most of them would make trouble when ever or where ever possible! That was how I wanted it as well. I made many "Jock" friends and shared many events with them.

This camp was another God forsaken, bug ridden dump! We were given a lentil soup which wasn't too bad. Anything is good when you are starving! Also we received one third of a loaf which was GREEN throughout with mold! It was impossible to cut the green out as you'd have no bread left, so one just ate it! Fortunately, we only remained at this dump for one day. What a surprise I got when I saw my pal, Ray, in this camp as well! They had come up by Red-Cross ship. Left after us, but arrived before us. Their boat was duly marked, hence they could sail more freely and come the straight forward route.

The following morning, after a sleepless night due to bugs and having to sleep on the floor without blankets, we were told to parade on the square at eleven am First and foremost for a head count. It was found that a few of the lads were missing. They had spotted a Man-Hole-Cover in the yard and, during the night, they lifted it and were away! Unfortunately for them, the lid had not returned properly and their start was not as great as they had wished. Never found out how far they got.

After the commotion we were given two loaves and one tin of meat between two. Bread. Not green this time! Hours later we were marched out with not a glance back at a place we considered was only fit for burning.

After a two hour march or should I say, struggle, through the town, we must have looked a right mob. Dressed in anything at all. Some unable to walk properly due to leg or foot wounds still not healed. Most weak from lack of food and all feeling ashamed at being subjected to such humiliation! Passing crowds of people en route. It suited "The Hun" alright as it lowered the image and morale of the British in a country where we were an ally.

Upon reaching the Railway Station, bound for, no one knew where, we had to wait for a couple of hours before boarding a train at 7pm. It was Monday, 25-8-1941. I know all these dates and events because of the diaries that I managed to write, hold on to and bring home with me in 1945. We were herded into cattle trucks. 34 men in each. No room to move. All doors locked with nothing to sleep on and nothing to put over us. We sorted ourselves out, lay on the floor, and waited for things to happen. This trip lasted eight days and eight nights! Another nightmare episode in my four years of hell! We passed through Bulgaria, Yugoslavia, Austria and Germany. Crossed "The Danube" a few times and the reason it was such a round trip was to avoid holding up their, more essential, rail traffic. We stopped at Belgrade and we were given lemon tea by the locals. They whispered hopeful messages to us in a slow subdued manner. I think that was the only time I smiled. Joy and laughter were but memories. Life was just misery and one became more and more miserable and downhearted.

During that rail trip we were lucky if they let us out once a day for issue of water and to relieve one's self! The longest they kept us locked up was 36 hours. Pure murder you can guess! We certainly called those "Huns" some names believe me! During one stop we, in our truck, managed to find an old can which the lads used to wee into and then throw out through the narrow strip at either end of the truck, retaining the can of course. When we were in a siding the guards would patrol along. We would wait till they were within a couple of feet of the slit and, if the can was full, we would sling the wee out hoping it would soak them. It did! As soon as we threw it we used to dive down flat on the floor awaiting a bullet through the siding. We used to enjoy hearing them cursing. It was our first bit of retaliation, but certainly not our last! Mind you ,some of the fellows objected to our action, but they were cried down and dived for the floor like the rest of us.

Through laying on the hard floor I developed a boil at the end of my spine. It gave me "gipe", but there was no treatment. When I did get it attended to at the end of the journey it was green with infection. The scar is there to this day! We rationed ourselves to two slices of dry bread per day. The meat had long gone! For, once opened, it soon went off. It was minimum eats and because of the lack of food many of the 1,000 POWs were taken ill but nothing was done for them. Everyone prayed for the trip to end so we could somewhere, get sleep and possibly a hot meal. Talk about the Altmark! This must have been even worse and we didn't get released like they did!

Eventually we arrived at a place called Lamsdorf on the Polish border. Everyone showing the strain in their faces, due to lack of sleep, lack of exercise and, most of all, hunger. We were marched to the Prisoner of War Camp, Stalag VlllB. After being searched (As if we had anything! If we had we would have eaten it!) We were put into a compound with brick huts and, of course, surrounded with barbed wire fencing plus gun turrets all around. The camp covered a large area and there were many Dunkirk lads there, having been POWs for a year or more. To our surprise it was announced that Red Cross parcels were in the camp! We were to receive a half parcel per man for four days on the trot because of our condition. This issue was allocated to us due to the Dunkirk lads foregoing their issue. A fine attitude and sacrifice to their fellow compatriots under the circumstances. It was unbelievable to see such food!I shared my parcel with Jim, my Marine pal. How wonderful to see such efforts being made in getting Red Cross items to the prisoners.
A marvelous organisation! One that, without doubt, kept many men alive. The Marmite in certain parcels was taken out and used for those with Beri-Beri as a vitamin to help cure them. We also got 50 cigs and what a great feeling it was to light up again! We made cups from the empty tin cans and ate till we were almost sick!

The following morning we were all de-loused, had our hair shaved off, given a number, which was put on a board in front of each one and our photo taken. Just like a convict. My number 22781. Still got the plate to this day! We were now registered and came under the protection of The Geneva Convention. On occasions I wondered just what protection we were covered by? As many incidents happened were those responsible were never brought to justice! The metal plate had to be worn around the neck at all times. If not punishment was the order of the day!

This was my life in my early twenties. Nothing to claim an Oscar for and nothing to help the pangs of youth. Just frustration upon frustration! Here was a body wanting to do so much, but was curtailed, tied up and faced with a bleak future. I can tell you, we all looked a right bunch with no hair. All our clothes were also de-loused at the same time but it didn't work, for in no time we were again infected and alive with lice! They did annoy! We could kill loads of them by hunting through one's clothes, but hours later it would be as bad as ever.

My pal, Jim, was in the wooden bunk next to mine. We shared everything together. One day, I recall, we were given a stew which contained: Potatoes, cabbage, prunes, dried fruit and Lord knows what! We ate it as beggars can not be choosers! Another issue was a kind of mint tea which a lot of chaps used for shaving water, or some would add, if they had, say cocoa to make a proper drink.

It was amazing what was made out of empty cans. The main item was what they called a Blower. It consisted of a long funnel with a tub arrangement at one end for wood, coal or anything flammable. At the other end was a round wheel and half way along, a fan driven by a shoe lace or even a piece of strong string. These items, as I say, were all made from tins. Empty, of course! They could generate terrific heat and would boil water in no time at all! Some of them were elaborate, streamlined and the pride and joy of the maker! "The Hun" guard used to stamp on them whenever they got the chance. Jealousy and spite no doubt!

At one time "The Hun" used to have guard dogs patrolling the compounds every night, which meant men could not go to the latrines after dark. So what a section of them did was to make rugged edges on tins, entice the dogs over with a tip-bit on the glassless window sills and as the dog jumped up they would lash out, ripping the face of the dog as hard as they could! No way was the culprit found as the windows used were on the opposite side of the hut to where the search lights were. Howls from the animals were to be heard all over the camp and guards would burst into the hut hoping to catch someone but all they would find would be a bloodstained can! In the end "The Hun" had to withdraw the guard dogs altogether. A victory for the POWs!

The latrines in each compound were very long bench type efforts which filled up very, very quickly and were alive with rats! After a few of the lads were bitten by these vermin it was a case of taking a can with you when you went to the toilet and putting your testicles inside to avoid rat bites! Not very nice but essential! We later received a blanket issue. Two each and that was a bonus for the nights were really cold as it was now mid-September. Before the blanket issue, I used to put the palliasse, which contained straw, over me for warmth. This place was also bug ridden and I became a victim once again. Because of this, and after a short spell in the Stalag, a number of us put our names down to be sent out on a working party. The reason was that it would be a new experience, food was more, or supposed to be more then we were getting and also they would force one out anyway. Although I had upgraded myself to full Corporal instead of Lance Corporal when we registered so I didn't need to go on working parties but I wanted to stay with Jim. Also it was to break the morbid fear of going mad with just laying about!

Then the winter months were not far off and if you can imagine that there was no heating in those huts. No glass to keep out the cold, Polish winds and we were right out in the wide open, wild country. It would be murder to say the least and who wants to freeze to death anyway! Besides it was hinted that typhoid was raging in the Russian Compound which was at the top end of the camp. They said many had already died. So. Move on was the best bet!

I had inquired about getting massage for my arm, but was told it hadn't healed enough and as these working parties were supposed to be for periods of three to six months at a time I reckoned it would work out right.

On the 15th September 1941, at 5am, we were allocated to a working party. Where we were going, we did not know? But upon being marched to the station and again put into cattle trucks, we began to regret our decision for we feared another nightmare trip! This time, however, the truck doors were left open with two guards posted inside. On the Tuesday morning we arrived at our place of work.

## Chapter 7
# First Working Party.
# First Escape.

It was still dark as the train pulled into a station siding and we
waited on the platform till daylight. Then we were marched off.
Having kit to carry, it wasn't easy.

Jim had trouble because of his foot wounds and I helped
with his bits and pieces. We arrived at a billet which was a
shambles! An old building, wired in of course and looking back,
what could one expect!! We were issued with two threadbare
blankets full of fleas! Gee! What a start!

The place was called Mittle-Langenau- Holenalbe in
Sudationland on the border of Czechoslovakia. The job
consisted of a quarry, lime kiln and railway station yard. We
were split into three groups and were picked out by the firm
bosses like cattle! A situation I unfortunately had to endure
many times during those four years.

I, with twelve others, were chosen for the quarry. Among
the party were Aussies, Kiwis and British. The quarry was about
an hours walk away which included about three miles up over
fields and hills. This trip was hazardous at the best of times, but
during the winter months of snow, hail and rain it was even
worse!

But still we had to go! The work was hard and difficult for
me and many others who had injuries.

At first the walk to and from the quarry was very
distressing for we were far from fit! Time helped as our early
days were winter, so the weather prevented us from having to
endure many arduous hours and as spring approached things
improved.

Many events happened during my period at this working
party which was named or called E 251. Particularly I recall a
chap named Alcock who was ill but yet forced to go to work
despite his protests and in the end he had to be rushed to a
hospital where he unfortunately died. It turned out that he had

shrapnel in the lung and treatment was what he needed but did not get! Who paid for his death? His funeral was a farce! Transported on a cart! Looks good on the photo but ,believe me ,it was NOT!!

On two occasions we destroyed pictures of Hitler! The first time, in the mess room up at the quarry. It was really cold. There was a fire place, plenty of logs for the lit fire in the civvies' room next door, but nothing at all for us!

One of the chaps said we could have a fire if we had some small pieces of wood  and a bit of paper to start it. The very next moment I saw the big photo of Hitler hanging on the wall!! Down came the picture! Used for paper kindling!! The frame for the small wood required! Logs on ! Great big fire ! Plenty of warmth!

Now, due to the fact that the removal of the picture had left a distinct mark on the wall, it was not long before all hell let loose! We were rounded up and questioned about the missing picture. Everyone kept dumb. We were threatened with a life of hard labour or would be shot! This, of course, was after  interrogation by the Gestapo! Still we all remained silent. So, after returning too and completing our quarry work for the day, we were marched back to the billet to be met with a hostile and rough reception! A few rifle butts to the body and made to stand and face an inside wall while the remainder of the men who were working at the Kiln and Railway were allowed to have their watery stew.

The Commandant was phoning around to see what should be done to us. About two hours later and, after being held in a position of attention, we were allowed to dismiss, getting our grub and relaxing after our ordeal.

It turned out that, after a long discussion between the Commandant's Superiors, they agreed that, as that room was allocated for prisoners, the photo of Hitler should have been removed! Success for us and a slight smirk for having released a little anger!

The second time we defaced a photo of "The Hated One" was on an occasion when we were made to go to the railway station on a Sunday to unload three rail wagons of bags of cement. The usual ten to twelve so called "Trouble Makers" were ordered out! Sunday was usually our only rest day but we were being denied that because of the 'Picture Issue ! After emptying the first wagon we were waiting in the rest-room for them to move the second into position when an Aussie jumped onto the seat, reached up and dragged another picture of Hitler down,threw it on the floor,jumped on it shouting "YOU BASTARD!"

Needless to say the glass shattered, but it didn't stop him inviting us all to have a go. We didn't take much persuasion and all took a turn kicking the destroyed picture and kicking it under the seat. It looked a sorry looking mess I can assure you! This time however not a word was mentioned about the incident and to us it was another feather in our cap. May be it doesn't seem much, but to us, under the circumstances that we were forced to live, it was indeed a triumph!

Trouble was far from over on this working party as food became scarce and there were no Red Cross parcels issued to subsidise the lack of wholesome meals.

We decided to meet in the late evening after we were locked up for the night and before we were cast into darkness to  discuss the situation. The outcome was that we agreed to refuse to go to work the following day and every day thereafter until they gave us more  and better food. The stews were mostly water with a few potatoes thrown in with their  skins still on! Mind you, if the skins had  been taken off there would have been less still to eat! Here we were going on STRIKE! A decision reached, not without a lot of argument, but in the end all were in favour.

Strikes were unheard of at any time in this country and never by prisoners!

There were thirty of us on the party and, as I say, all agreed to support the action. The plan was to get up as usual the following morning then, when the whistle was blown for us to go out into the hallway to collect our boots, put them on and parade outside, we would not move. The second whistle blew· Meaning late comers needed to hurry out. To our surprise and disgust TEN of our so called colleagues walked outside and paraded for work!! We twenty remained inside. The action of the few did not help us at all but we stood our ground and explained why we had taken such a decision. Despite the threat of violence we refused to alter our agreed plan, hence the few outside were marched off to work and we herded into a room and locked in.

A short while later the guards opened up and made us remove all the kit out of the room including our palliasses. Everything, until the whole room was bare. We were herded back in again and locked up. "Jerry" was going mad! He tried everything to incite us, even taking the few cigs that some of the lads had received from home. We were not given any food nor drink but we put up with it all and soldiered on ,making the best of things. The ten returned from work but wisely were kept away from us! They got their meal, but we remained locked up. Receiving nothing. We had to sleep that night huddled together for warmth. It was a long night with little shut-eye between us. Dawn broke with us all really, really hungry, but no matter. We had committed ourselves and stick it out we must! Immaterial to what the future had in store.

After the traitorous ten had gone to work we settled down to a morning of wondering what this second day of our strike would bring.

To our surprise the door was unlocked and we were invited to carry all our kit back in. Also palliases. Given a stew and allowed out to shave and wash! What was the catch we thought!

What plan had "The Hun" in mind to get us to drop our action! Nothing was said and we were duly locked up again. This time with a few comforts. We slept well that night or should I say from the moment the door was locked!

Day three, when there was only one guard left in the billet, he came to the door, knocked and shouted through the door that later that morning they were sending a contingent of troops from the main barracks with a top Officer. He advised us that if asked, as you have been each day, to return to work. Do not say a straight NO, but say you WILL go providing you are given more and better food. Good advice we thought and we agreed to follow along those lines. Gisler was the guard's name and he was helpful to us on a number of occasions. He was young and had done a stint on the Russian front.

Sure enough, an hour or so later, with plenty of commotion, the door was unlocked and we were marched outside, lined against a wall with a line of soldiers facing us with rifles by their sides! This made us think! We muttered among ourselves that it was very unlikely they would shoot us out of hand. The top Officer stepped forward and asked for a spokesman, Johnny Cosgrove from Manchester,we had agreed would speak for us as he had learned good German and could understand everything that was said. He did, in fact, say to the Officer what had been relayed to us earlier by Gisler. The Officer said "Your ten colleagues that are at work, when interviewed, had said the food was alright."

We doubted that. He also said we should have complained

to Stalag first before taking such action independently and causing so much trouble. He advised us that he had inspected the food situation and would be sending a report through. He finally pointed out to us that such a thing as a strike was punishable by long terms of hard labour and so he gave us an ultimation saying, that if we were not out within ten minutes with our boots on ready for work, he would send the guards in to sort us out with a heavy hand.

We were dismissed and wondered inside. We started to discuss our predicament. Was it a bluff? Should we take a chance and hang out? Time was flying by! It was agreed that if they were serious then some of us could be really hurt and we didn't want that to happen to any of the twenty brave men who, against all odds, had taken a step which must have been one of the few times such action was seen in Germany! We duly rushed and got our boots as the ten minute deadline was rapidly drawing near. Out we went, laces undone, lining up facing the steel-helmeted soldiers who now had fixed bayonets!

We were marched through the village with all the locals, now well aware of what these Allied Prisoners had done, watching through windows and doors, nervous and possibly more frightened then we were at seeing so many troops in their small community. On up we went to the quarry, arriving to be met by abuse from the foreman, Joseph Hammercheque and his colleagues that made up The Ten!

Needless to say they got a mouthful and were told where to go in no uncertain terms. The outcome was indeed better food eventually, but bitter resentment against those ten.

It is true to say that those weeks prior to the strike were starvation periods beyond explanation. Although we could hardly walk we were literally driven and forced out each day. I had, as promised, learned myself enough German to voice my disgust and utter my abuse at each and everyone when ever I felt that way inclined! This rebellious attitude of course landed me in a lot of serious trouble many times, but at least I had a certain amount of satisfaction despite the bruises that followed. The statement about returning to a Stalag after three to six months was just a complete lie! And fellows were fed up with the heavy work everyday, hail, rain or snow!

In the quarry we had to break the blasted stone up, load it into skips which were sent down on the overhead cable to the kiln for burning. We got up to many tricks to delay this process which was helping the German War effort. We'd break a very large stone that would be so heavy it would take take all of us to manhandle it into the skip. When dropped in it would jam solid into this container. We'd then send it down the overhead wire system to the kiln where other prisoners would wheel the skip into the ovens. The local German civvies would unload the quarried stone straight from the skip. When they came upon a jammed skip it meant a lengthy holdup and a backlog of skips blocking the line which was forced to stop and gave us the opportunity to sit down, rest for a few snatched moments and listen to the shouts of all and sundry about sabotage etc! These comments went in one of our ears and quickly out the other!

We would, at times, force the skips to fall off the machine on leaving the quarry hence a further long holdup and another welcome rest for us! Life for the foreman, Joseph, was one long problem. He would try the soft touch, which worked a little, but when it came to the hard stuff, he got nothing but abuse and less work done. If that was possible! He seemed to have a soft spot for me as on a few occasions he would give me a slice of bread or perhaps a bit of cheese. I remember one particular Christmastime he gave me some writing paper and envelopes, which later got me into trouble.

The Engineer also had his problems, for a word out of place would result in him being called all sorts of names by us POWs. It became a regular thing for us to be reported to the Commander on our return back to the Billet. He would threaten us but, no way, could he stop our daily periods of mischief! All in a good cause as far as we were concerned!

Escapes from the work party had taken place sporadically and so it was a short time after they had transferred me to work at the kiln and on Tuesday 29th September 1942, having been there for over one year, I decided that I'd make my first break!

Sam Weller, a chap from my unit, and whom I'd remet in the hospital in Greece was on my working party and he decided to accompany me on this quest for freedom! He was a Londoner, and when on "The Hellas" a bullet went through his tin hat, raced around the inside and came out through the same hole and straight through his hand! How's that for luck Helen!

Back to the story. It was 1:45am. We'd broke for dinner. The guard had got cocky and disappeared somewhere although he was supposed to remain to watch us. Neither Sam nor I had planned anything or prepared ourselves for an escape!

It was a spur of the moment job! Besides, we were really

fed up with everything.

We crossed the road and sprinted off up over the fields into the woods, intending to make a densely wooded area before 1 o'clock when we'd obviously be missed.

Now, unfortunately we were unaware that we'd been spotted by a local civilian working at the factory while we were crossing the road! He had informed the authorities that a couple of POWs were on the run! We did spot someone approaching in the distance but, thinking he was a farm worker and not knowing that the wheels were in motion against us, we carried on. As we advanced nearer to him and he nearer to us we realised it was the foreman from the quarry armed with a rifle! He had been notified by phone from the factory that we were heading that way. He halted us and in no time we were surrounded by Huns. All with guns cocked! We were marched back to the mess room at the factory and locked in!

After a short spell the door opened and in came the guard who should have been on duty guarding us! He immediately started to knock us both about with his rifle butt. The party Commando then arrived and he too started hitting out with his dress bayonet. We kept getting knocked to the ground and, like mugs, kept getting up each time, only to be grounded again and again! What kept us from retaliating I don't know! Perhaps it was that we spent too much time on the floor!

In the end we stayed down only to receive the boot! We eventually came out of there with plenty of bruises and plenty of cuts and were made to work as usual but now with a guard following our every move. Upon returning to the billet that night we received a couple more blows and we both ached all over.

At around 7pm that same evening a guard turned up at the billet and Sam and I were ordered to pack our kit and move out within fifteen minutes! We were taken from the lager (our camp) and about a mile or so up the road we met another four lads who were under guard. This group of four were transferred over to our team of two. It appeared that these four had also attempted to escape from another working party close by.

All of us were being transported back to Lamsdorf-Stalag where they had a section specially equipped for those who committed an offense. The punishment was solitary confinement, bread and water etc. We boarded a train and arrived there at 3pm the following day only to be told an hour or so later that "The Bunker" (jail), was full! This compound was where the Russian POWs had been and where the Typhoid epidemic had broken out. Those remaining Russians who were not stricken by the disease were moved out altogether late 1941, early 1942.

The guard who brought us was due to go on leave after dropping us off but he was ordered to take us back to where we came from. Now, as this guy had a date with his girl friend in Breslau, he decided,after some discussion that we'd go with him, stay the night and travel on the next morning!!

When we arrived in the town he tried his best to get rid of us at a local barracks but they refused to take any responsibility and turned us all away!

It was, by then, 9pm so the guard decided to take us, six of us, to his girlfriend's flat! We all rolled in and she was all for us bunking down there for the night, but the guard reckoned he'd be in trouble if seen and reported. By then we were starving with hunger but no food was on the horizon. We all then left the flat. Girl-friend as well! We were made to walk in the gutter while she and he walked on the pavement. He took us to the local rail station hoping for success in pawning us off there. The station master agreed to lock us up in a store room while the guard and his girl went back to her flat.

The station master found us some bread and a warm drink and we got our heads down as we were worn out completely! Most of us were in a deep sleep only to be awoken because of the movement of Jews and Russians on the station.

Believe me the treatment of them was scandalous! They were continually beaten and battered. Not only adults but young children as well! No wonder the Jews have so much hatred for the Germans! I witnessed such treatment on a number of occasions that harrowing night! It even happened to women with small babies, elderly women and men loaded with their worldly goods thrown over their shoulders! Due to the cruel and unrelentless beatings they received, these goods would fall to the ground and remain there till kicked into some siding away from the desperate owners! Who would ever of thought that people could be so humiliated and degraded! Little did I realise the full horrors of what I was witnessing that night !

Our guard turned up later on looking quite pleased! He had to endure many comments from us all on his romantic escapade! We boarded a train and alighted an hour or so later to be marched to the barracks at Trautemam. Again the Company Officer refused to have us! We were getting fed up with all this messing around and were beginning to show our displeasure to everyone that came in sight! We were roared at from all angles but somehow no one appeared to want to strike out at us! Perhaps it was because we had not shaved for a few days and looked more like a bunch of dangerous rogues! Hungry ones to boot ! After a further long wait it was arranged for us to be sent to a Civvie Jail some distance away.

# Chapter 8
# Civvie Jail And More To Come

We arrived there at about 11pm Thursday 1st October 1942. My first experience of being locked up in a cell. A proper one at that. We were split and put three into each pit. It was about twelve foot long and about eight foot wide with a shelf type arrangement at one end for sleeping on. It had no amenities what so ever! So we just lay down and quickly fell asleep. About 2am we were awoken and given something to eat and boy, were we glad of that! Long had gone the days when breakfast was early morning, dinner at mid-day, tea around 5 or 6! It was a case of eats when ever and if ever available. At six am we were woken up and given more soup which was quite thick and hearty. Surprise, surprise! Two eats in four hours! We agreed we'd stay if this was the pattern!

As the day went by we talked about the New Zealand Sergent that we met at the Trautenau Barracks. He was sentenced to two years for striking a guard. We hoped he had done a good job on him and we reflected just what could have happened to us had we retaliated in that mess room!

At around 2-30pm in the afternoon a guard from our working party appeared on the other side of the bars. He had come to take Sam and I back. We went mad but could do nothing about it! So, about 7-30 that evening we found ourselves back at working party E251.

It was work as usual the following day with a very close eye kept upon us! We were thoroughly browned off!

A few days later Sam and I were informed that we were to be sent for a further four days "straffing" (punishment). So, on the 7th October 1942, we started to march to a place called Spindelmukle. Way up in the hills. After about 5 Kilometers we stopped and, to our surprise the other four lads that we had shared the cells with in the city jail joined us! So we all set off on another ten mile stint. We kept stopping and smoking. Much to the annoyance of the guard but we knew what was coming once we arrived! And besides, he wasn't sure if we would turn on him should he say too much.

The journey took around 5 1/2 hours. On arriving we had everything taken from us. Just what we had guessed! Sam and I sat down on a bench in this office only to be immediately roared at to get up and stand to attention. A bright start!

This place was a very large Russian Lager. Way, way up in the hills. Full of Russian Prisoners of War, who at that time, were parading around, completely in the nude! The reason being that their clothing was being deloused! But, as you can guess, it was really cold! So wide open and so high up!  We were put in a small room about three floors up. Just the  two of us. No bed. Bread and water only! The other four were above us as we could hear them moving about.

We were taken out for exercise once  per day and, as the Russian POW's passed "The Huns" on guard they had to salute them each and every time! This was expected of us as well but we very impolitely told them where to go and no matter how they yelled, we refused point blank! As usual we stuck together over this and, in the end, the Officer accepted our reasoning when we said we are British and do not salute ordinary soldiers in our army and we won't do it here!

The Russian Interpreter there was OK. He slipped tobacco under our door and we enjoyed a sly smoke! The bread issue we scoffed all at once! Washing it down with the water. Sleep was a problem as the floor was rock hard, but we managed a couple of hours a night.

By the Sunday we had completed our time and, as we had to wait till the Monday for the guard to take us back, we were given our cigs and also a hot stew which was very welcome as the weather was really cold! Beds, too, were given and that night. Perfect sleep! So endeth the results of my first escape attempt. But it wasn't to be my last for this working party was still getting me down!

Christmas 1942 came and went without alteration to the monotonous way of life!

We tried ,amongst ourselves, to imagine it was Christmas and to remind ourselves that that was another year gone! Family was very much in the mind! What were they all doing? How were they all keeping? How much longer must we be parted? Now two years! Will 1943 bring release? My sentence was never ending and the outlook- Not good!

The news, bad for Britain, was conveyed to us regularly by "The Hun." Spirits were low indeed and one felt worse at such times. Pure depression! The only thing that possibly kept us sane was mail from home. How one looked out for it! It was the only link with civilisation! The only way one could believe that you actually belonged to someone! You became such a loner and longed for home and loved ones.

Day after day.

Week after week.

Year after year.

There was no end to this suffering and heart-ache! When mail came for others and none for you, you felt neglected, lost, not wanted. No one knows just what a letter meant nor how you reacted when you were left out! A letter received was read over and over again! Living the moments that it was written! Counting the days since it was written and praying that everyone was still keeping safe and well.

Among the 32 of us on this working party there was an Aussie in his mid forties. Quite refined and rather religious. Every Sunday evening he would hold a prayer and hymn gathering for anyone who wished to attend. It was something that did help the upset you felt. I looked forward to it anyway. New Year came and went.

They did give us a very small white loaf each and a bottle of beer! Neither went down too well as our thoughts were many many miles away. The days were very cold! The snow heavy and often. We were made to clear snow some ten foot high through the main street! Boots leaked, feet soaked and many suffered from frost bite with ear lobes chipping off! It was so cold that even urine used to freeze!

This billet only had an outside tap for washing purposes. It was left running in the winter to avoid freeze up! Lads used to get washed with their Balaclava Helmet on! In other words they would just rub around the area that was visible. Sometimes not even that and who could blame them? They were going nowhere!!

# Chapter 9
# Second Escape Attempt

The winter months slowly went by. Spring was coming. Warmer days and milder nights.

So it was that on the night of 25th May 1943, I, with three others of my colleagues, made another break from this working party and a possible chance of complete escape from being a POW. For this time we were more prepared.

Over a period, we had saved the chocolate from our Red Cross parcels. Believe me this was hard to do for food parcels were not a regular issue! They would come, say for one or two months, then none for three or four months! Bare German rations were then all we had to live on and, at this particular time, it became very hard not to dive into the choc-bars which we were trying to save! But when one decides to make a break then you need to make an effort! Hence our determination to save the chocs!

This again wasn't easy as many searches of the billet and of ourselves were held at regular intervals. But luck was with us and we found ways of fooling our captors and retaining our provisions!

In addition I negotiated, with difficulty, a brand new 1943 map of Czechoslovakia. I talked a Civvie into parting with it and also bribed others with cigarettes! Next we needed a compass! Now, as it was impossible to obtain one, we made our own! This was done with three sewing needles and an army trouser button.

First, you magnetise the pointed end of the two needles. This we did with a big magnet that was in the workshop of the quarry. When there was no one about we'd make an indentation in the hollow of the button with a nail. This protruded from the four holes and you then put the two needles through the holes so the magnetised ends touch. You rest the whole lot on the thread end of the third needle. Hence it swings to the north. The beauty of it was it could all be dismantled and carried on ones person without suspicion or detection! I spent the winter months preparing and making the necessary equipment for the escape. This kept me motivated and looking forward to the future.

Our way of escape had been used many times before by a number of the working party lads. First, we would be climbing into the loft of the building. You see before we came to this billet, a brick wall had been built in the loft space which served as a barrier to the rest of the buildings and from the area we were in. The loft door in the ceiling was over the place where I slept which was on the top tier of a long bench arrangement. It was covered with brown paper to avoid detection. Why? I don't know. For that was the first thing we investigated upon arriving over eighteen months earlier!

At one period the roof started to leak and got worse and worse until "The Hun" called in a firm to repair it. The workmen knocked the wall down in the attic space to gain entrance to the effected area. Instead of going in from the room when the job was finished they did not rebuild the wall! This we found out by exploring months later when locked up at night.

We awaited the first opportunity to put our escape plan into action. First thing on that morning of the 25th May 1943 when our jailers would open up the doors for us to wash and get ready for work, we would already have exited through the open loft space and we would be poised to cut through the barbed wire with clippers which we'd pinched and kept hidden just for this occasion! Upon roll-call, when it was discovered some were missing, a search would immediately take place. The hole in the wire would be discovered and "The Hun" would be under the impression the escapees had only just gone, when in fact we had quite a few hours  start!

Needles to say, "Jerry" was very puzzled and very concerned, as responsibility for escapes were held against the guards and Commander and the punishment for them was usually a transfer to The Russian Front!

About six breaks were made through  the roof before ours. It later turned out that the lads who had gone prior to us (a month before) had, when captured been forced to admit to the method being used. Fortunately this information did not occur until the day of our intended break and was not conveyed to the working party Commander until the late morning after we had gone! The lads did cut the wire and caused panic amongst the guards until later on when all was revealed.

It was about 11 pm. All were supposed to be bedded down

for the night. We removed the brown paper from the loft access, pushed up the wooden cover and were duly helped into the loft with words of good luck and good wishes. Besides our eats, we had a rope to lower ourselves from the roof once we'd made our exit from the loft window which was about ten yards from our point of entry. As it was pitch dark we had to be careful not to put our foot through the ceiling! We kept close together and passed any information back along the line in hushed whispers.

The plan was to keep our boots around our neck. Mainly because there was a wide brook at the end of the building and it was about 10 foot across, with about a foot or so of really cold water from the surrounding mountains flowing down quite fast. We had discussed the possibility of shouting out. "Bloody Hell! It's Freezing!" As we entered to cross to the other side.

We negotiated the loft successfully and out on to the roof. The moon was shining as we slid to the gutter to make sure everything was clear. But to my horror! There was the guard patrolling on this side of the building! And even worse was to happen, for, at that moment the Commander appeared, torch in hand

My first reaction was. Did they know of our escape? Had they been tipped off?

There I was. Unable to move! The adrenalin flowing madly! Unable to inform my colleagues of the terrible position that we were in! They were becoming impatient. Wanting to move, to get away from the immediate surroundings, yet the two Huns stood talking for, what seemed ages. At least they were not aware of what was just above their heads! Had he swung his torch up, he would have seen me quite clearly, one foot in the gutter, trying to make myself as flat as possible. Holding one end of the rope with my mates holding the other, waiting for me to drop to the ground.

I fully expected them to shout out at any time. The tension was unbearable!

But they must have been also aware that things were not right for at no time did they make a move or utter a sound, although later they said that they were ready to return back into the loft had I hinted of any detection! Believe me, we were all full of fear! After all, being in that position is no joke!

After what seemed like hours the Commander moved off and, seconds later, the guard also moved to patrol the other side of the billet. We didn't bother with the rope. I just dropped to the ground. The others following in seconds, knowing there was no one close enough to hear the thuds!

Next, the freezing water and up the other side into the fields with not a murmur between us. I think we were either too scared or too relived. We literally ran across the pastures until we were completely out of breath. An odd glance back showed the guards' torches shining out into the darkness, unaware, at that time, they had lost four men! We put our boots on and continued our journey in a more leisurely manner discussing the earlier events and even joking about them! But, as I said, it was no joking matter at the time.

Now, it was our intention to make our way towards Prague for it had been hinted to us that an organisation existed in a monastery close to the town who would help prisoners escape out of enemy territory. We were not sure of this but as we were deep into occupied countries it was worth investigation. We continued to walk throughout the night, distancing as many miles as possible between us and the place we had left behind.

Daylight soon broke and that meant, eat a little, sleep a lot! We found a dense wooded area which was ideal! Head down. Relax and dream. Every noise would alert us. Birds singing, a rustle in the trees! Voices way in the distance. 1 think exhaustion won in the end, for we did manage a couple of hours and needed them!

We continued our journey at dusk, using the compass to great effect and heading in the right direction. Staying, as much as possible under the protection of woods etc.

All went well till the Sunday! For, as day broke, rain started and it simply poured down ,causing us to look for alternative cover other than the woods that we were in, as even the trees were shedding rain through their leaves! After descending down, we spotted a large unused sand quarry and explored it till we found a small cave area which was just big enough for us to shelter in. We'd been there an hour or more when the rain began to get lighter and we agreed to give it another half hour or so for things to dry up a 1ittle. We settled down to a further smoke.

Then, all of a sudden, a civilian appeared from nowhere! At least we didn't see sight of him until he popped his head around into the cave. I think he got as big a shock as we did! He said his greetings and we quickly tried to pass ourselves off as French, for they used to work in different areas, even different countries and roamed around as they pleased minus guards as France had capitulated. After a chat, and some minutes later

,this man bid his farewell and off he went, although he seemed to accept what we said.

We did not waste time in getting back to journeying under cover in the woods.

Walking as far to the summit of a hill, as possible. Shortly ,we realized our suspicions were correct, for in the distance, we could hear the continual whine of dogs pulling on leashes and eager to do what was pretty obvious! As the noise came closer we could now see some dozen or so men carrying rifles, making their way into the woods via the sand quarry.

At this point, one of the lads decided he wanted to crap. Possibly because of fear. He carried out his act using some of the chocolate paper for the finish. We then scuttled as far as we could under the heavy bush growth. Splitting up and yet staying fairly close. Slowly but surely the voices came nearer! The dogs' whines more and more frightening! We lay very still, not daring to breath!

Then, all of a sudden, a shout!

"Choc--a--lard--paper!" We knew they'd come across the disposal job and knew we were not far off. At last they were right in our area, even stopping, not a couple of feet from our hiding spot! How they did not spot us I'll never know! Luck was on our side! They moved on. We breathed a sigh of relief as voices and whines became less and less distinct.

It was now becoming dusk and the posse party were descending, leaving us to ponder over our ordeal which had lasted for hours and we were fair worn out! No sleep and what with the fear of being discovered it made us feel absolutely exhausted! Once again we decided to move on and down the other side of the wood. Upon reaching the roadway that ran between the wood we were in and the one on the far side, we were in for a further shock! To our dismay there were soldiers patrolling. No doubt convinced we were trapped there till dawn! Their system was for one guard to march from the centre to the right, while the other guard was marching from the left to the centre. This went on for a good half hour or more, with us watching and waiting, wondering if this was the end of the line. Were we really trapped?

Unable to talk beyond a very low whisper, we were considering returning back the way we had come when suddenly our patience was rewarded for the guard who was nearest to us, upon reaching the centre of the road remained there until the other guard arrived! They started to chat and that was our opportunity!

One by one we sneaked across into the adjourning wood,and away! Up,up as far as we could, feeling smug at having out smarted "The Hun."

Let me say to you ,dear Helen, that escaping was not a picnic! It indeed was a nerve wrecking, heart stopping event! The tension was terrific! Every movement we heard was treated with suspicion. Every rustle of leaves brought uneasiness and even your mates' voices, suddenly asking a question, caused the blood to flow that much faster!

Why then, you may ask, bother to breakout at all? Well! Adventure, and the fact that one's youth was wasting away and one needed to do something to prove that life still held some sort of challenge. That, I feel was the answer. Still, here we were with a grin on our faces and looking over our shoulders just in case!

Eventually, after a couple of hours, we emerged from the wood. It was a moonlight night with occasional cloud blackening the sky and shrouding our journey. And as such a night had helped our exploit across the road so it became our downfall!

About 4:30am the following morning, we had to, according to our compass and map, make our way across open fields and along country lanes if we were to get nearer to our target of Prague. We were doing this when, all of a sudden, a team of about ten Home Guard Members, pounced out of the darkness and we were surrounded! Unable to dash or even move! Rifles were pointing at us and we were told to march on! Now, due to close supervision ,I was unable to unload myself of the map and when we arrived at a hut in a small village nearby,we were duly searched and ,of course, the map, plus money that we also had, was discovered.

This caused a terrible commotion! Especially as the map was dated 1943!

Everyone there more or less panicked! Phone calls galore! Then, silence! We all looked at each other. Then questions, questions and more questions! We had, during the earlier rumpus, renewed our agreed plan not to reveal the information that they obviously wanted. So, as they made no progress this meant a further trip to a Police Station!

Our continued silence there caused an outburst with my pal, Jim Gomery, a lad from Liverpool, getting a crack over the head with a cane! We were then informed we would have to

*My mother, Lucy Clare O'Reilly at age 14 in Dublin. Circa 1908*

*An early family photo–Mum, Dad and my older sister Eileen. Circa 1919*

*My mother Lucy Clare at the time of her engagement. Jan. 1914*

*"The Tower", New Brighton. This burned down in the 1920/30's*

*One of many poscards sent by my father, Thomas, to my mother whilst they were courting. Circa 1913*

*My father, at the helm of one of his ocean going vessls, 1920's*

*A postcard showing Castle St. in Liverpool. Circa 1908*

*The back of the postcard sent over to my mother in Dubli (As you can see my father was a man of few, if any, words). 1908*

*A view of "Overhead Electric Railway and St. Nicholas Church", Liverpool. 1908/09*

*"The Landing Stage", Liverpool, 1909*

*The back of the postcard sent over to my mother in Dublin (As you can see my father was a man of few, if any, words). 1908*

*Receipt for dads engagement ring, Jan. 1914*

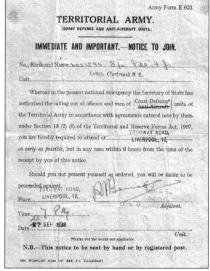

*My notice to join the Territorial Army, 1938*

"The Hellas", the royal yacht that was commandeered for our evacuation from Piraeus Harbour, Greece in April 1941. This was the ship that was bombed by enemy planes and resulted in my capture and wounding.

POW's Dream—from the war years newpaper, full page.

Newspaper cutting announcing my status as a P.O.W. Aug. 9th 1941

This P.O.W. tag had to be worn around the neck at all times. Stalag V1113.No. 22781

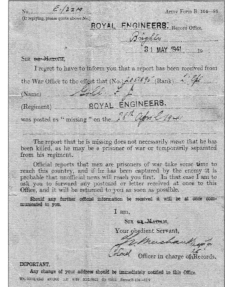

Notification on 31st May 1941 that I was posted as "missing". It was another four months before my family was aware that I was alive, though a POW

Some local curency that I acquired whilst a P.O.W. (not worth a carrot!)

*10th May 1945 – My telegram to my parents to inform them of my liberation and imminent return home.*

*Madge and I enjoying time together after I was demobilized – post war years.*

*Our complete and happy family in the late 1950's Trish (L), Lorraine (M), Helen (R)*

*Our annual pilgimage to Kalamata and a memorial service held in the town park (Frank, 2nd row, 3rd right)*

await the arrival of the Gestapo!

We were all knackered, what with no sleep, starving with hunger and all our cigarettes taken from us! We felt rough! We were made to sit on a narrow bench and, if we started to sway with sleep, we were immediately clobbered over the head in no mean way!

After a long wait two members of the Gestapo, plus an army high ranking Officer came through the door. After consultation with those present, they proceeded to grill each of us separately in the hope of finding out where the map, etc, came from? As I said, we agreed from the start that no information of any kind, no matter how any-one tried, would we divulge where or how we came to have the map. It was important, not only to us, but also to the Civvie that had supplied it.

As I was the one who had the map when caught, I was taken in first. The room was bare except for a single chair in the centre. One of our Army officers stood by the closed door. I was told to sit on the chair. One guy stood behind me. The other in front. At first they spoke in a quiet mode, asking where the map had come from? Who gave it to me? Each question, I answered in a negative way. Then their voices rose to intimidating shouts! At the same time the guy at the back pulled my head back by grabbing my hair and the guy in the front stamped hard on my foot! Still shouting. As the guard at the back released his hold on my hair, my head fell forward and I received a back hander across the face from the interrogator in the front. It was then that the British Officer intervened and said. "This man is not a Russian! He's English! He is protected by the terms of "The Geneva Convention!"

This interruption to their blows seemed to divert them and they shouted at me " Get Out!"

As I staggered out one of them kicked me up the backside. The other lads suffered the same abuse at their hands.
It was now well into the morning and, upon reflection, we found we had in fact traveled some fifty odd miles and were, thanks to our compass,heading in the right direction for Prague, but unfortunately we had again failed. The compass was not discovered as it had been dismantled into needles and a button! (Who would know these basic commodities were such a sophisticated tool!) As we remained tight-lipped it was decided that they would return us to the same working party in the hope that the map provider would, upon seeing us, reveal his guilt!

'This did not happen as the individual involved hated "The Hun" as much as we did and was continually carrying out acts to disrupt them. I'm sure that guy was deeper into things, maybe working in a resistance movement, than he ever gave the impression he was. Later he thanked us for our efforts in remaining silent despite the grueling and cruel treatment that we had to endure. If it had not been for the presence of the Army Officer, during the interrogation, the Gestapo would have adopted the heavy handed method for he kept a sober outlook and, on occasions, intervened. We all agreed that, as we discussed it later, it was indeed another rough experience and "THIS WAS MY LIFE" at the time.

We were tried and sentenced to seven days in the Bunker (Military Jail). Bread and water, with one hot meal each third day. The sentence was light for me as this was my second attempt! Perhaps they forgot! Anyway, it was the beginning of another period in my captivity, Helen ,and if you are not fed up with all this I'll continue!

# Chapter 10
# Jail, Then The Coal Mines

Each of us were in a separate cell. It was cold and although there was a round fire in the middle of the floor area, it was not lit. Jim found that he could lift out the bar that was holding his cell-door closed. This he did and soon we were all out into the main area which was duly locked from the outside.

Using straw and wood from the cells we lit the fire and were enjoying a warm, when suddenly the door flew open! Too quick for us to get back inside our cells, so we were caught and suffered a few belts with the rifle butt and a threat of no hot meal when it was due and we'd only been in the place an hour or so! This sure looked bright!

We soon found that one of the guards was indeed a Frenchman who had joined the German Army upon the capitulation of his country, France. We first of all, when he was on guard duty, asked him to bring us in our tooth brushes which were in our kits in the barracks. This he did and when we further asked him to bring us in our cigarettes he refused. But when we threatened him with reporting him for his previous act of suppling us with tooth brushes, he hurriedly agreed! Hence we enjoyed a puff when ever we felt like it. We had to make sure that smoke traces were not lingering in the air when the usual guards were visiting to check that we were still there!

We continued to release ourselves when ever there was a lull and re-lock ourselves into the cell nearer the time of the regular guards' visits. While out we found that there was a Russian section of prisoners at the end of the block that we were in. We knocked out a wood knot in the dividing wall and used to converse with them, exchanging cigs for a little bread to help us to make our endless days more intriguing!

The French guard caught us one day making contact with our Russian friends but due to the blackmail hold over him, he did nothing about it!

The days passed. The hot meal came and, before long our confinement ended without any further trouble.

So, on the 8th June 1943, we were released and taken, once more, back to working party E251.

Working in the quarry had for sometime been done on a shift basis. Start at seven am. till one o'clock and then one till six. This was at the rate of filling a certain number of skips per shift. They had taken the men away from the factory and put extra on to break up the stone. Food was becoming scarce again.

It's times like this when, ravaged by hunger, you lay down on your bed and eventually fall asleep. Waking up about three or four in the morning with severe stomach pains and unable to fulfill your desire to eat until your bread issue before departing for work. It's a terrible experience and makes one frustrated beyond words! Ones hatred for your captors becomes worse and when you show it you end up with a rifle butt in the chest or back. Painful, to say the least, but does not stop the continual verbal attack from defenseless prisoners! That was our only weapon, verbal retaliation!

Since our escape the guard on the billet has been doubled! Seven guards day and night on duty. You couldn't turn without there being one right beside you! They were concerned and worried that someone would disappear! They must have been warned of what would happen if they did not have a full complement at all times!

My 24th birthday came and went! No one knew and the longing to be home and amongst loved ones grew much more intense. These occasions raised your anger and depression until you almost go mad with the thought of such an uncertain future.

Invariably, one would retire to one's bed and cry in the secret of your blankets!

It was on the 3rd August 1943 that "The Hun" decided that the men on the working party would be moved! The 28 of us, branded the trouble makers, were detailed to work in a coal mine, while the other 12 were sent to lighter jobs!

At first, I was on the light party job, but they soon altered that and accused me of placing myself in that section. I didn't want to be with that shower as all my mates were going to the mine and, like Bert Hutton, way back before leaving "Blighty", I too wanted to stay with my mates.

We were, once again, sent in cattle trucks. Usual mode of transport! To Krakow in Poland and then onto one of three mines in Katowice. Knowing the rough, hard work of being down a mine, we were examined by an English doctor who took no notice of wounds or physical weakness etc! We were all  pronounced fit to work underground. I don't know what he got out of it or what he had going for himself, but I do know he was called some names on that occasion!

On Monday the 9th, we were down the pit at 6am having been aroused at 5am.

We would get back on the surface at around 3:30pm. By the time we showered, it was dark again and we never saw daylight at all! There were many dark days of trouble.

First, Jim and I were given a massive skip to fill in a seam that was only a foot higher than the skip! The pit was full of water and every time we lifted a shovel of coal on a shovel nearly as big as the skip itself, we'd be soaked as we had as much water as coal on it. Not only that, but with the first shovel we knocked our lamp into the water and were searching around in the dark for it! When we did find it, it wouldn't light with being wet.

We were then transfered to another gang, filling skips in a larger area. There was a big Canadian Military Police guy among the fellows and as soon as we filled a skip, he would say, as we pushed it towards the main line for transporting to the shaft. "All push to one side!" With the result that the skip would jump the line and every time we'd lift it with a bulk of timber to reposition it on the track, we'd throw it too far over so it jumped the line again and it keeled over on the other side! As no guards were allowed down the pit we were guarded by a Stiger. A guy who carried a revolver and was one bastard! He'd let fly with a bullet and, needless to say, we did not try that particular escapade again!  They did say we had to fill 60 skips before we could finish our shift. We refused, but were told we would stay down in the damp, dark depths until we had completed the assignment! We took 15 hours to do this and then had a half hour walk to the cage at pit level. When the cage reached the top we stepped out to be met with rifle blows and boots going in as well! A couple of the lads retaliated and were beaten unmercifully! The rest of us took our bruises to the showers with us and the unlucky lads staggered in later, literally covered in blood!

On that day, there was an American soldier with us. He had come over to England and joined the RAF. He was shot down over enemy territory and taken prisoner. In Stalag V11B there was one compound for RAF personnel only. They were not allowed out on working parties. Now, what they used to do was swop with a soldier –Name. Complete identity, in the hope of having an opportunity to escape. I recall this American, upon coming into the showers after also receiving a  battering, saying. "God dam it! The things I do for England!"

I made up my mind to get away from this job, E 587, as soon as possible.

I found that, after I had been wounded in Piraeus Harbour, my arm was weakened and tender from the hard work. I'd put a bandage around my wrist at night and in the morning I found my whole hand had swollen up due to the bandage being too tight! For a while after the bandage was removed my hand resembled a claw and looked pretty incapacitated. Within an hour the bandage marks had disappeared and all was almost back to full working order! So here was my chance of getting away! After a couple of days trial, I reported sick and was duly booked to return to Stalag. Before I left that job, I recall incidents which may seem far fetched and perhaps, unbelievable, but are, in fact, very true.

There was a lad from Liverpool. Name of Moss. He had come from the quarry job with us. He was so desperate to get away from the trouble and stress of the mine that, one day when he was down the pit ,he decided to climb the shaft in a bid to escape! It took him well over an hour and, of course, he was missed from his section. When he did reach the top "The Hun" was waiting for him! Need I say what happened next! He wanted away from the slave labour of those mines. One evening he put his little finger on a block and chopped it off with an axe that he had pinched from the pit workshop! This act certainly took some courage but his determination was so great that pain meant nothing! Can you imagine, Helen, doing a thing like that!

Shows the bravery of the man! Many years later, I was in a Transport Cafe in Aigburgh, Liverpool, when I spotted, who I thought was this lad, Moss! I waited till I could see he was minus a little finger and I knew it was him! We had a good, long chin-wag about those rough, hard, sickening days.

Other chaps, and there were many, deliberately poured boiling water over their hands or feet in an effort to get back to Stalag! Some succeeded, but eventually "The Hun" realised and the victims were kept in hospital in the camp until recovery. Then more work down the mine! I did hear later that the M 0 informed the working party that if these acts were continued he, upon returning to England, would have those men put on a charge for self imposed injuries! I ask you! I personally knew a couple of the lads that went through the torture of scalding water and, as you can guess, they suffered a lot of agony! One lad, whose name comes to mind, was a New Zealander, Locky Sweeney.

At last, on the 23rd August 1943, I left the working party, E-587, en route for Stalag. Three weeks down those horrendous mines was far too long believe me. Everyone wanted away from the mines. Guess I was lucky! Only regret I had was leaving my mate Jim there. I felt sorry for all the men who had to work down pits and, as I had seen what went on, I knew just how much they must have greeted the Russians when they came through and liberated them from this living hell!

Upon arrival at Stalag the usual took place, searching me for any suspicious objects! They took all my mail off me and burnt it in front of me! I cursed them with the little German I knew. My reaction was also a distractory tactic to avoid them finding the diaries that I had concealed! Somehow I always managed to get by with them never being detected. Hence, I have them to this day and as I said I can relate dates, places and events just by turning the pages.

In the main camp I met many of my friends and was put again into the top compound. I mated up with a chap from the Seventh Cheshire Machine Gun Regiment, captured in Sicily. His name was Lol Tilley. Stalag VIllB was indeed a notorious place for it's many acts of reprisals carried out by the Germans on our Allied prisoners.

I recall the time after Dieppe, when the French Canadians had handcuffed the German prisoners during the battle. "The Huns", after hearing about it, decided that they would handcuff all the British POWs! So all in the Stalag were manacled! The set up was, "The Hun" would go from compound to compound and the lads would have to queue up each morning and "The Hun" would lock the cuffs on. There was about a foot space chain between and one could do little throughout the day. Movement was so restricted! The cuffs were taken off in the evening and refitted each morning. It wasn't long before some of the lads found ways of removing the cuffs! Some threw theirs over the wire. Others, down the toilet! But the favourite and the one that forced our captors to stop this foolish idea was as follows:

The daily queue had to enter in one door and, after being secured, the POWs would exit through a door situated at the

*A Letter to My Daughter*                                               *81*

other end of the hut. Now, as soon as the cuffs were fitted, one would go out through the exit door and when away from our jailers, remove the cuffs, go back, climb through a window and thus rejoin the line! This meant the queue was never ending! It was quite a while before "Jerry" realised just what was taking place. It was then accepted that it was a farce and soon stopped.

I saw, in that camp, two lads shot as they attempted to climb the double wiring that encircled the camp. They had no chance of escape and shooting them was unnecessary! You see, the lads used to make a brew christened, "Jungle Juice!" It was lethal, believe me! It was made of prunes, raisins and any other fruit that came in the Red Cross Parcels. It was fermented with yeast obtained by means of bartering and pinching! To make matters worse, boot polish, Brasso or anything with a trace of alcohol in was used! The stuff was so potent it would blow your head off! It used to drive lads mad if too much was consumed.

These two chaps had done just that and they wanted to get away. They could so easily have just been recaptured upon landing on the other side of the fence! It was not easy to climb the wire for there was a gap of say, five feet between the fences so they were never going to get away and their escape attempt was futile! Who paid for their deaths, I ask ? Another chap. A Scotch lad, who became tanked up with "The Juice", started to fight his mate. He hit him over the head with a lump of wood! Thinking he had killed him and filled with bitter remorse, he too started to climb over the perimeter fence and suffered the same fate!

There was even a distillery erected and in use! This was made from empty tin cans. Marvelous! I saw it working and was in awe of what a man is able to conjure up and produce from only begged and borrowed materials .
Many escape tunnels were dug and lined with bunk bed boards.

It was amazing just what did take place in that camp! At times POWs, who were wanted by the Germans for various offenses, serious ones at that, would dye their hair to avoid detection! I recall one prisoner wanted for some criminal misdemeanor, being recognised by a guard. The guard chased him through the camp. He tried to turn into  one of the huts to evade his pursuer, but tragically lost his footing and tripped. He was shot at point blank range and in cold blood! MURDER!

Clothes were made for official escapes. Passports and all sorts of documents were painstakingly produced to help all those brave men who were inclined to attempt an escape.

Mostly, these were arranged for Royal Air Force prisoners who were needed at this stage of the war, back in Britain, as they were skilled pilots who risked their lives daily to attack the enemy targets on the Continent

Of course, it was not widely talked about but we were all keenly aware that our whispered plans may be heard by our captors and the attempt could be foiled. Many false tunnels were dug to put "The Hun" off the scent of the "Big One" that was the route to freedom for a selected few of our fellow prisoners. A number of these decoy tunnels often collapsed just outside the perimeter fence or be discovered when the regular searches were made.

I remember in one compound the fellows there made a brew of "Jungle Juice" especially for "The Hun" to discover. This brew was a lethal concoction that the lads had enhanced with their own spit and urine, cigarette ash and cigarette ends, to state just a few of the mentionable deposits! All thrown in to complete the hooch. Sure enough, it was found and carried down to our captors' quarters for consuming at a later date! Hope they enjoyed it!

"Wide boys" in the camp started swop shops. There were many to choose from.

Others put their skills to use producing Plays or Shows on makeshift stages. On special occasions we were able to see Fancy-Dress-Shows. They were put on with parades through the camp. The costumes displayed were marvelous! All made from whatever could be scrounged.

Football matches also were put on as there were many professional footballers who were prisoners. England, Scotland, Wales and Ireland would play in a League. Also, there would be other games played on a regular basis. Even Yankee football was played and, on one occasion, they put on a show called. "One-Hundred-Men-And-A-Ball". Fifty guys on each side! What a lark! One never saw the ball once the whistle went.

I was receiving massage at the camp hospital for my wounds. This went on for some weeks until they said no more could be done until I could get a skin graft. The arm didn't seem any better despite the massage and to finish the treatment did not really worry me.

The camp was greatly overcrowded at this stage, for a large number of British POWs from Italy were pouring in as "The Wops" (Italians) were slowly but surely losing. These prisoners were already captured before we had even reached Greece and it was "The Hun" that decided they should be shipped to camps in Germany.

This was indeed encouragement to us as we felt that the German stronghold in Europe may have been weakening and we thought things were starting to look brighter. There became a big Typhoid scare at the same time as these extra prisoners arrived. So, on the 17th December 1943, I again went out on a working party.

This time a railway job in Hindenburg. The billets were good. Coal fires and hot water. I had my first full bath since Egypt in 1941. It was great to soak and one felt a million dollars after the luxurious soak! The first night there saw two lads break-out and get away. That caused some trouble but we didn't mind for by now, we were used to and accepted our enemies' reactions. It was all in the game and was what we lived for.

After a couple of weeks there one member of the party died. Again the funeral was a disgrace! His family would have been so upset!

Christmas came and went. On the Boxing Day evening the billet ran out of coal. There was a big mountain of the stuff across the railway lines not far from where we were but the guards would not themselves go and commendire some, fearing the worst. So we talked them into allowing us to climb the wall and pinch a load! They agreed. A guard tagged on behind just in case we did a bunk, but it was far too cold for that! We all enjoyed a nice, warm few days off work. 1944 arrived. Again hoping this will be the last year of captivity. Browned off!

Nothing was getting any better. Depression became worse year by year and one would feel like giving up altogether, but it was a case of hang on and see.

Once again my German got me into a beating for my pal Lol, who could not speak any German at all, got me to call the guard a real mouthful for something that happened a couple of weeks before. As we were working on the line outside the main station we asked to knock off for dinner. The offended guard lifted up his rifle and let me have it, quoting the remarks that I had previously made. Still I didn't mind as it got rid of some of my built up hatred. What was a few blows anyway? The idea was to grin and bear it.

The Scotch lads made another "Jungle-Juice" brew. Boy did we go to town! They were in a right state and I recall that two of them were intent on going down and setting about the guards! Some of their compatriots put an end to that by laying these two out cold! Just as well otherwise it could have been curtains for us all! Mail was still the only thing to keep one sane. We were allowed to write home and to friends regularly. Whether they all arrived was another thing! The job E 552 was now becoming a real trouble spot and many of the POWs went on strike to protest about the appalling conditions. As a result, what's new! Blows from rifles were a common occurrence. Escapes became a regular event and all in all, it became, once more a scheming effort to get the hell out of it!

We would do little or no work at all. When working on the main station we would encounter German civilians who would be waiting for their trains on the platforms. We'd just lean on our shovels and pass derogatory remarks about them, mainly out loud. This, of course, got the Foreman going mad as he had to get a certain amount of work done a day and our philandering was wasting the German War Effort. We would not go along with that and needless to say the trouble was constant and relentless.

We used to call the Foreman "A Ten Pfennig German!" For he was, in fact a Sudaten German. This would incite him no end and I can see him now fuming with his great mustache twitching madly! What a guy and a grumpy one at that!

I, again, managed to work something out and on 11th May 1944 I found myself back in Lamsdorf, Stalag V111B having worked my head and used my wits to secure a return trip to this particular camp. I met many of my friends again. We had plenty to talk about and I found myself once more in the top compound. It was a little like being back amongst your family. A family of persecuted and incarcerated prisoners far from home and loved ones!

# Chapter 11
# The Invasion And Events At Stalag V111B

On June 6th 1944 we heard of the invasion of Europe. Radios had, over the years, been smuggled in and in one compound hut they even erected a large map to follow the wars progress! Despite regular raids and searches all these items went undetected.

At last, things were looking brighter. Everyone was talking about home. Everyone appeared to want to talk whereas before everyone looked down in the mouth. I started to play football in a five a side team and while playing one day was unfortunate enough to break my left wrist. Unlucky that it happened to my wounded arm! It was three days before I could have it x-rayed, set and put in plaster. I spent a few days in the hospital. Then out, to struggle through ,once more minus the use of one arm! This went on till mid-October when the plaster was removed.

The events were just as previously stated, in the camp. A number of lads were shot, unnecessarily and in cold blood!

News was good, but slow, by our standards. We were so impatient to see an end to this life of misery. Air raids were plentiful. The sky darkened by a thousand Bombers going over at one time and quite often! The planes were piloted by Americans of course.

Food was becoming more scarce. Our German captors becoming more and more frustrated.

It was on the 20th December 1944 that they ousted us out of our huts at 7am and kept us stood on Parade till 5:30pm! It was freezing cold! We had nothing to eat or drink as they searched around looking, not only for lads who had broken out of the internal Bunker, but also because things were not going good for them on either Front and we were the target for revenge. That day was called by us, Black Wednesday, and even to this day my pal in Newcastle, who was the person I shared with at that time, reminisces on it if we exchange letters around that date. Geordie Bell is his name. Ossie, to be exact.

Another Xmas came and went. 1945 was now here. Was this to be the long awaited year of our release? Things sounded better and hopes were aroused. We could even hear the Russian Tanks getting nearer by standing in the slit-trenches that we had dug and as you bent down you could hear the rumble and feel the vibration of the ground. We now felt we could soon be in Red Square, but unfortunately "The Hun" had other ideas.

I, at that period, was feeling more depressed than usual for it was in late 1944 that I heard through a letter from my sister, Eileen, that, Joan, my girl-friend had broken off our engagement! Now news like that is bad enough when you are among loved ones who share your upset and offer help and encouragement to get over the shock. But when you are alone and far away it is considered a knife in the back. I was not the only one that this happened to. There were many. In a lot of cases, wives going off with other men. I recall many husbands threatening

violence and retribution upon their return home. I wonder how many did resort to such action? Mind you, in my case, if you read through my diaries you will see I had written an entry that related how I had dreamt that Joan and I would break up. Perhaps it was because, at that particular time, it had happened to someone else and it was on my mind. Or may be it was a premonition, but what ever, it was soul destroying to say the least.

I realized later that such events are inevitable at times of war when people are parted for such long periods, but believe me it certainly does not help the morale under such circumstances. Anyway, one had to soldier on and overcome the setbacks of life.

At that moment in time things were beginning to happen and, as I said, we were awaiting the arrival of The Russian Army. But as gun-fire came nearer we were told that Stalag V111B was to be evacuated.

There were around 12,000 men in this camp with over 1,000 in each of the ten compounds! They started to empty one compound at a time. Going from one side of the camp to the other and so on. We were in the very top compound which ran right across the whole area and were the last to be evacuated. Now, in-between each compound there was a dividing wire fence and a large gate which was duly locked each evening.

Given this window of opportunity, many of us had, over time, cut holes in the wire. They had never been repaired, so we decided that before "The Hun" came to clear our compound we would go through the wire into an empty compound and hide in the huts to await possible liberation. About 100 of us did the same and all went well until we decided to come out of hiding. To our surprise there were, in all, about 4000 lads from all the compounds who had all shared the same idea and had done the same!

It was a case of seniors taking over in case of raids on the Cook-House or riots and looting by our own Brothers in Arms! I recall a complete Glasgow Razor Gang being among the crowd. They had done some fine work during the previous years by going out on working parties where some POWs were working beyond the necessary expected quotas. Thus aiding the German War Effort. These hard men would intimidate the errant POWs by threatening them with severe reprisals if they didn't slow down and do as little as possible! These gangs, who operated on the wrong side of the law back in Britain, believe it or not, did keep law and order in the camps during those long, dark days of incarceration. Everyone towed the line and everything was on an even basis with us all feeling that the end of this "Hell on Earth" was very near.

Sanity needed to be maintained by those who had outwitted the enemy on their own ground! As no German guards were around it felt great! Unfortunately, the gun-fire became less and less until there was no action at all. We had been convinced that the nearing gunfire represented Allies who would soon find and release us. We wondered had "Jerry" packed in or had the unthinkable happened and the Germans had managed to overcome our fellow soldiers!

It was now a week since all were marched out and lo and behold, we were confronted one morning with the return of some guards! It appeared the thrust had been driven back and our presence had been discovered! So we became, once more, under German dominance and put under Marshal Law.

Food was scarce. Water- non existent! We would collect buckets or tins of snow and thaw it as best we could. The weather was terribly cold. Everything was disrupted. No mail. No news drifting in. I missed my letters from Mum and Dad and from Eileen, who had, during my captivity, got married. From Madge and from friends in general. It was a dead end completely! A set back! All our hopes of celebrations in "Red

Square" were now just a faded hope! We kept warm by burning the remaining bed-boards, doors, anything at all that was flammable! At least in winter the bugs were not as bad and that suited me for the dread of being eaten alive by those pests had not disappeared.

Towards the end of February, without warning, we were rounded up and given five minutes to move out! What a rush! But we didn't have much anyway. We were marched to the railway station and put into cattle-trucks once again. Forty three people to each carriage. We got one hot soup in ten days! No hot drinks and remember, it was the depths of winter! No form of heating in the trucks.

It was Hell! Many lads broke out and jumped while the train was still in motion!

Air Raids were regular occurrences. We were lucky many times during that trip. Danger faced us from friendly as well as enemy fire!

Eventually, we arrived at a place called Hammelburg, which had a camp numbered Stalag X111C. A dump to say the least! No showers. No beds. Crowded into barracks with no lights. No Red Cross parcels, but plenty of snow. Air-raids every single day and planes, by the thousands, flying over at night as well!

One particular day the soup issue at mid-day was condemned by the British Medical Officer in the camp as inedible! He said it was unfit for human consumption due to hundreds of maggots floating on the top! It was a case of refuse to eat and continue to starve or take your share, remove the maggots and eat. Thats exactly what we did!

The whole place was really terrible and to make matters worse a further concern arose about the possible outbreak of Typhus! The camp was greatly overcrowded and it was decided that for the safety of all, it was best to get as many POWs as possible out to work on farms etc in the surrounding area. So it was that I, with about twenty other lads, found ourselves in a small village some distance from Stalag XIIIC. We were put in a billet and the following morning the local farmers came to select the ones they fancied to work on their land.

It was again like a cattle market and we were less than pleased! These sort of jobs were mainly filled by the French and it was only because the situation was becoming more difficult that we, British, were being used.

During this period I was still mates with Lol Tilley. We wanted to work together but the policy was: One man per farm for obvious reasons. So we had to split up. I was on a farm where two girls were living. One single. One, the wife of the farmer who was away in the army. We had to work on the land during the day and return to the billet at dusk. We had our meals on the farm during the day. This was a change and the comforts of a home helped to brighten life a little. We could have a joke or so while in the farm-house but as soon as we came out all had to be dead serious, for the family could not afford to be seen to be fraternising with the enemy!

We had been working there for about a week or so when loud gun fire could be heard in the not too distant vicinity. On returning to the billet in the late evening the two Germans in charge of us had orders to move us out.

## Chapter 12
# Third And Last Escape

Now these two guards had been drinking prior to our return from the farms and it was late at night and pitch dark as we started to march to God knows where! After we had gone some mile or so, the two tipsy guards decided to walk together at the front of the party instead of one back, one front. Lol and I, who were at the back of the section, decided to drop off and hide up.

We were still on the outskirts of the village and after staying under cover for some half hour or so we moved out and as we turned a corner a short distance away, bumped, slap bang into three fellows! The shock was heart stopping until we realised they were also from the party and they had made a run for it, the same as us. Some short way after we had jumped the prisoner group, we joined up and made our way along the country lane towards another village. Soon we could hear the roar of motor vehicles approaching! Unable to take cover, we just remained where we were and on came a number of trucks full of German troops!

The first truck, upon seeing the outline of humans, pulled up and asked if they were on the right route to such and such a place. Fortunately, one of our five could speak German like a native and he just instructed them without really knowing where they were going or really caring if he sent them in the right direction or not! Just whatever came into his head! So, with a "Heil Hitler" they all shot off into the dark and we shot off the other way as fast as we could.

It was an eventful night. For some mile or so further on we were confronted with three or four Home Guard type of persons. Elderly men with rifles. Memories of my last capture sprang to mind. We immediately took the offensive and, as the gun fire was still going on in the distance, but not as much, we politely told them they'd be better off going home, throwing their rifles away and remaining in doors! They thanked us, wishing us well and took off. Luck was with us on this night alright.

We noticed a farm house across the fields with a very dim light showing so we made our way to it in search of somewhere to hide up and wait as events began to unravel around us. When we arrived we saw a large barn looming on the horizon. We entered. Going up into the loft among the hay and there got our heads down for a few hours sleep before dawn.

The noise from the hens woke us and we explored the barn where we were. We found eggs and enjoyed raw eggs for our makeshift breakfast which went down a treat! The gun fire had, by now, stopped completely. We found out, very much later, that it had been an American Tank Raid upon Frankfurt which was repelled by the Germans.

We remained hidden in the loft, watching between the cracks in the wood structure, any movement of the farm workers. Once or twice some of them came into the barn but never ventured up the ladder. We decided that, at night fall we would move out and continue our journey in the hope of meeting up with the British Army!

It was about 4pm on that day, we were lying down awaiting dusk when we were aroused by all sorts of movement and activity around the farm. On looking out we saw, to our utter despair, a complete German Battalion moving into the farm area.

It had earlier been notified to all prisoners by the German forces that escaping was at this moment in time no longer considered a joke and would be punishable by a firing squad!

Our outlook seemed bleak and there was now no way out!

To make matters worse they moved the Headquarters Section into the barn below us with office furniture. The lot!

We sat watching from the loft and waiting for the next move, which proved not to be too far off for, after about an hour, up the ladder came a soldier with a palliasse, intending to fill it with straw and then grab an hour or two of sleep. As his head appeared we greeted him in a polite manner.

He duly descended the ladder without a word and without any straw. He made his way out of the barn not stopping to talk to anyone! Now, as nothing immediately happened, we thought that may be they were of the opinion that we were French. That impression did not last long for as we looked out of the cracks we saw armed soldiers surrounding the barn!

Our immediate reaction was to build a wall of bales of hay around ourselves, double thickness, in the hope of smothering any gun-fire should it come. Mind you my motto still remained. If I'm born to be shot I won't be hung! Still, like my colleagues,

I took cover. Shouts of."Come On Down!" were voiced from inside and below us. We remained where we were despite the increase in the volume of the commands and the curses of all those below! We were not soft enough as to show our faces without being sure that a bullet was not going to be the outcome!

Eventually, we spotted a further two ladders being set up and within seconds we were surrounded with rifles pointing at our heads! Farm workers, armed with pitch forks, pick axes etc, encircled us. This helped to make the event look anything but a tea-party!

The Commander bawled out so much, so fast that we couldn't understand a word! Not even Snowy, who was good at German and who had saved our bacon the night before when we encountered the convoy in the village. When we did manage to get a word in edge ways, we coolly spun a yarn that we were working on local farms in the area of Bad-Kissingen and, upon return to the billet we found that the guards with the remainder of the working party had left. So we had moved out hoping to catch them up! But as it was impossible to find our way because it was going dark, we had found this farm, going into the barn and intending to see the farmer in the morning. Exhaustion had overwhelmed us and we had fallen asleep and did not wake until the arrival of the troops.

Of course "The Hun" was convinced that we were Paratroopers, dropped behind enemy lines and this meant long interrogation complete with body searches and kit scrutinised! This sort of thing we were used to so it made no difference at all. To prove that our story was correct, they decided they would take us with armed escort, back to the village which we said we were working at. Upon arrival, although dark, we were taken to each farm that we had been on and were duly identified! After leaving the villages the pressure was eased as we five were taken to the billet in which we had slept prior to our break away. As this Battalion did not want us around, they sent for a guard to take charge of us while we continued to do farm work. So one could say another shot at getting free had failed. It brought its scarry moments, as you can guess, Helen and perhaps makes for interesting reading for you.

Our reign did not last long for within a couple of days a further guard arrived. One hundred and fourteen soldiers to be precise. We were roused out of sleep and told we were marching. All my pre-planning, for just such a situation had been dashed by the unearthly hour of the disturbance! I intended to take to the hills and hide up, with the girls bringing me food etc. I even spun a yarn to the guard about leaving some of my kit at the farm in preparation for this escape. Unfortunately he agreed to accompany me. We did go and wake the girls up. Obviously I did not have any thing there, but I had to pretend as the guard was with me. I only had a chance to say a quick goodbye and then I was marched back to the billet. I must have been crazy to expect the guard to let me go alone! But it was worth the risk.

There were now eight of us, as some others, had been returned to the village as well. They were rounded up just after us. Thinking back, those two drunken guards must have ended up with very few prisoners by dawn the following morning or when they reached the railway station, which ever came first.

This time there was no way of escape possible for we were closely watched by the guard and any ideas of absconding were just not even to be remotely considered! We marched and marched till our feet were killing us and, of course, we kept lagging behind until, in the end this guard decided to buy a small cart from a farmer which we could put all our kit in. Two would pull while the others just strolled along. We would take turns and then it was the case of those pulling the cart lagging way behind!

The guard couldn't win what ever he expected of us! For when ever he started to become a little awkward we would threaten to sling his kit off the hand-cart and he'd have to carry it himself. This quickly altered his approach to us and he became more and more to understand our way of thinking! He even traded some of his cigars for some of our remaining Red-Cross parcel items, like cocoa or coffee. Even a blanket that one of us had! We would even force him, upon entering a village, to go and beg, borrow or steal bread in the local bakery. We now had this guy completely under our control and as we, the party of eight, were of mixed nationality, namely; one Welsh chap, one Irish, two English, two Aussies, and two Scotch, the guard would say, one of you pretend to be a New-Zealander, and when I go into the bakery I'll say that I have personnel from each country. An International approach could prompt sympathy and, more importantly, bread to keep us alive until our hoped for liberation! Don't know if it worked or not but he invariable managed to produce a loaf to help feed us. This guard was in fact now on his own with us. The other chap had long since left. Where he went we didn't know or care. For he seemed a rigid swine and that would have meant trouble galore for us rag tail prisoners.

One of the lads developed terrible blisters covering the whole of both feet. We got two tree branches on the shoulders of four of us so allowing him to put most of his weight on the branches and less on his feet!

We came upon a town and instructed the guard to find a hospital as it was impossible for this chap to continue. The pain he was suffering was killing him! A hospital was found, but they refused to admit the lad who said he just could not go any further. They wouldn't even dress his feet or attend to him at all! So, after some discussion amongst ourselves we decided, with the approval of the chap in question, to just dump him and take off with assurances that we would send our liberators to tend to him. So we left him inside the hospital doorway and ran away, round the corner followed by the bumbling guard shouting "You can't do that!" To which we replied "Alright you go and get him and carry him!"

We turned and continued our journey with the guard in hot pursuit going on about what would happen to him and how our reckless actions were going to be the death of him and us too!
Again our response was "Shut-up or your kit goes off the cart!" That did the trick!

Wonder what ever happened to that poor chap! Left alone with no one willing to help. At least his feet got a rest if nothing else! Self preservation can result in some cruel and heartless reactions!

At nights we were locked up in some barn or other, using the hay to keep warm while the guard would try getting us and himself food from the farmer.

Our main aim was to delay as long as possible, from joining up with the main body of POWs marching towards Austria. We knew that that would mean less of everything and many more guards to cope with.

We went through many towns which were absolutely razed to the ground from Allied bombing. In the town of Nurenberg we had to stay in the railway station over night. The bombing was continual and troops were on the move all the while. After a lull in these procedures we all slept a little on the stone floor and when we awoke we found that our kit had been rifled and items were missing! The guard, who had gone off somewhere after dumping us in the charge of the Military on the station, had left his case with us but that had not been pilfered so we immediately broke it open and took back the items which we had earlier traded with him. When he arrived we said, look what your colleagues have done! He cursed, but later kept on saying "I'm sure you lot took my stuff!"

This was because we flogged the blanket for some bacon at a village farm that we were passing through and when he saw us eating it he became suspicious as to what we had used to barter for the food. We kept denying but he wouldn't let up. The wheels on the cart kept collapsing with the weight of the load and this poor guard was frustrated hunting around for new ones. As usual, the threat was to dispose of his case first! We also threatened not to move until the cart was mobile.

We had been together some ten or more days and eventually we did catch up with the many, many thousands of POWs. We must have covered some 300-350 kilometers on our trek! Our fears and misgivings were obvious! Food was non existent! There was always the promise that, at the end of a day, if we kept marching, the Red Cross "White Vans" would be there to provide us with sustenance. Needless to say these life saving vehicles did not materialise as our guards were just saying this to keep us marching!

The Red Cross had introduced these vans to provide relief to the POWs and they provided parcels because there was no German food or supplies. What a wonderful organisation and there is no doubt that they, the Red-Cross, had kept us all alive during our term of imprisonment. For, without those parcels, we could not have survived at all! Many prisoners suffered from Beri-Beri and most from malnutrition! Myself included!

I recall that I got into an argument over this insistence of the guards to build up our hopes of nutrition, only to have our hopes dashed at the end of a grueling day when we would find there were no vans nor food to be had! The guard was in his late fifties and could speak good English. The lads that knew me kept shouting "Go ahead Frank, tell him!"

In the end the guard said "Do you realize, that if I had been a younger man and with what you have said and called me, I would have shot you!"

Talk maybe, but I didn't challenge him any further.

As the column was slowly grinding on, the front section of prisoners would leave the road and explore the contents of a field. It would be seconds only before the thousands would be on the field leaving the place completely bare, if of course, there was any stuff which was edible! Shots would be fired over our heads in an attempt to stop us but no way would anyone leave until all had been foraged and cleared.

Mangle stores (Cattle-Food) were raided and we would continue our journey enjoying this turnip-like veggie! Again, if we stopped at different farms for the night it was common practise to chase, catch, kill, pluck, clean and cook the fowl for food. The farms were left practically, henless by the time we moved out!

Eggs were stolen by the score and if vultures had descended on those farms the places could not have been cleared any better. We were fortunate, in as much as, as we marched, we were always, either just before or just after the continual bombing of all the towns we passed through. Not so the contingent of Officer POWs that we came across. They gave a number of us cigs and we chatted for some time. Later they were dive bombed by our own planes, killing about fourteen and wounding about forty. At least thats what the "Jerrys" told us! What unfortunate luck! We crossed "The Danube" and went through Mainburg on towards Munich.

On we went into Austria and it was here that our long overdue liberation took place.

## Chapter 13
# Liberated! Home At Last

We were spread out into farm barns around a large mountainous area and after a couple of days we woke up one morning to find the guards had disappeared!

A gang of lads took off after them, threatening that they were going to kill as many as they caught up with! Never heard if they were successful. Hours later we spotted American tanks traveling along the road. We all rushed down to greet them. Everyone had tear filled eyes and hearts filled with the joy of possible freedom at last!

The Yanks gave us cigs and food and we chatted for a while. Then their Officer asked us to remain where we were till later and not to impede troop movement by clogging up the roads. We went back to our barn and just lay down relaxing with the knowledge that, at last, after so many years we were free. Well almost! At least we knew things were moving along.

The feeling was difficult to absorb. We lay low for a while, but decided to go and look around the area where we were based. Our new found freedom was pulling at our insides! We needed to move and be on our own. It was not long before we came across a couple of Polish lads who were working on the local farms. Not from choice I can assure you! They had acquired rifles and we soon realised were also partly drunk! They informed us that they knew where some of our enemy were hidden. We jumped on to the cart that they had and as we raced on they shared their drink with us. We did not find anyone at all, even after searching a few houses! Reckon they, "The Hated Huns," must have taken off as soon as The Yanks were passing through. We left the Poles on their journey of revenge and destruction and returned to our sanctuary - the barn.

The following morning one of the lads. A Greek, was out side having a wash, when a single shot rang out from the distant woods. The unfortunate man got a bullet right through the neck, killing him outright! It was a sniper. Possibly one of the ones the Polish chaps were wanting us to find. Enough was enough. We were not going to take any chances. It would certainly have been a tragedy to get through years of captivity only to be killed in those first, heady days of freedom ! So we collected our kits and pulled out on our own. Four of us! We had covered about 800 Kilometers during that long march, a further few miles would not matter.

We stopped at a hotel, demanded a meal and a room and spent the night there, in a proper bed believe it or not! We also feasted on a grand meal which was served without any questions or payment! The next day, while continuing our journey through the town, we were picked up by some Yankee soldiers and taken to one of their camps where we were fed beyond words! The result was that I paid for the over nourishment of food, the like of which I had not tasted for years! I was ill for a number of days. Felt terrible! Even watching my colleagues eat made me feel even more nauseous! But, gradually, my reaction cleared up and I, once more, was able to digest food, though I picked at my food in small doses.

The Yanks, after a week or so, used to take us to a local air field near Mannheim each day and set us up in groups to await the arrival of planes. If the aircraft were returning to Remies empty then the pallets would accommodate a number of us, if we were lucky! Many a day we'd return to camp until the next flight flew in.

After a couple of days sitting in the sun on the airport tarmac, it became our turn. Boy, were we lucky for the plane we were allocated to was flying straight to Oxfordshire. So we didn't have the problem of any further wait in France. What excitement and joy it was to be on this troop carrier heading for England and proper freedom at long,long last!

The feeling was one of indescribable elation! The years of being locked up and treated like scum were now over. We considered that we had suffered beyond endurance and I know that no way would I allow myself to be put in that position again. I would not live through those years ever. I do know and agree that those unfortunate lads taken prisoner in Japan and the surrounding areas of the Far East, were far, far worse off than we were. I know that they were treated like animals by the Japanese, unable to retaliate as we had opportunity to do. My sympathy goes out to all those chaps and I know that my condition and situation in Europe was no where near as bad as those Far-East POWs but to be put into a position such as we were in is a miscarriage of justice and should not happen to anyone! To lose so much of one's life, youth and so much freedom is soul destroying and it leaves a scar for the rest of one's life. Nothing can alter that loss and it remains a very deep hurt.

So, after a comfortable flight across France and The English Channel, we landed back on England's safe shores. I had been away five years in total and four years, to the day, that I had been taken prisoner.

When I was released, many additional things happened which I have not written about as it would have taken much, much more writing and much, much more paper to complete. Besides, I reckon you'll be well fed up with this load of rubbish if you ever get this far! Your mind will boggle and your glasses will be worn out Helen. Poor you!

Mind you, I still have some forty years of life left to write about, events and memories, so that we are up to date and into the mid 1980's. That part of my Post War life will take some time to write about, but not near as much as those first twenty six years when I grew up and lost my youth all those prisoner years!

We were taken from the plane to an army camp. Given a thorough medical, a complete delousing, less the removal of our body hair this time. Thank God! Fitted out with new uniforms. All documentation was completed. We were fed and billeted for a couple of days, then given a warrant to travel by rail, with indefinite leave, to our homes.

What it meant to go one's own way, with complete freedom of movement, was frightening indeed! You kept looking over your shoulder and expecting a rifle butt in the back or a voice to command you to halt. The fear that your freedom was but a dream and not real at all haunted you. The mind had been troubled for so long that you could hardly accept you were among friends and that everyone was your friend and ally.

Here I was, on a train, sitting on an upholstered seat. Not in a cattle truck! I was heading for my Liverpool Home. My Mum. My dad. My family. Tears of joy consumed me.

What would it be like after all these years?

What changes would I see?

So much was occupying my mind but most of all I just couldn't wait to see my loved ones again! The train could not go fast enough! Every stop was Purgatory. Every mile seemed a yard! Oh. Roll on Liverpool! At long last, we pulled into Lime Street station.

The place was alive with Military Police! I alighted from the train with jacket open. No Cap on. Just thoughts of home. When, suddenly a voice boomed out from the platform "Corporal! At least fasten your jacket!"

A pleasant voice, so I just did as I was asked and quickly headed for a taxi. Had that M-P been the slightest bit aggressive in enforcing strict military dress, I fear I would not have made it to the taxi rank. Rather, I would have been marched off on a charge. I did feel that these personnel knew, possibly by the new uniform and possibly they had been tipped off that such attire linked with emaciated men meant we were prisoners returning to our loved ones.

So I traveled the last few miles to the place I had longed and prayed to see for so very long and dreamed about so very often. I recall stopping the Taxi in Liverpool Road, by "Lodges Newsagents" and walking down "Kilnyard Lane" towards my home. Half way down and on the other side of the street, heading my way was our dog, Spot. A black wire haired terrier with one white area over one eye. My family had got him after our other pet, Peter, had to be destroyed. Spot became a great friend and a real member of the family.

He, upon seeing a person, crossed over and smelled and without me saying a word, that dog just went mad! Jumping up and down until I stooped down and held him to me. He licked away at my face. His tail going wag after wag. God, that was to me an unforgettable moment! What a welcome from a loyal and adoring companion! Picking up my kit, I completed the remaining steps home and was surprised to see written on the wall in Big letters "WELCOME HOME ERIC AND FRANK!" The whole of "First Avenue" was decorated with flags and bunting. The neighbours had made a great effort to welcome us home. It was such a nice gesture.

As I opened the back door leading to the garden, my Dad came rushing out and we both embraced. Hugging and kissing with tears of joy flowing unashamedly. Then my dear sister, Eileen, came into my arms with a repeat performance of never ending hugs. No words. Just pure emotion. All the while I'm watching the kitchen door awaiting the appearance of my dear Mum, but she didn't come. I said "Where's Mum? Is she out? When will she be back?"

God, how I longed to see my dear Mother! How many

times I had needed her during those dark years and now my heart was pounding for this moment. I wanted to greet her and see her dear face again. I always carried a mental picture of her in my mind. With her lovely brown eyes smiling and willing me through those long five years of horror and incarceration!

No one answered me. My Dad said "Come inside son" The house, to me looked wonderful. Everything as I pictured it many, many times. Spot was still showing his delight and I just felt overwhelmed with joy and relief. No one knows how I waited and longed for this moment! All I needed now to complete my world was the one person who was missing. I again asked the question and my Dad said "Sit down, I have something to say to you."

He then told me that my mother was very, very ill upstairs in bed. My immediate reaction was to dash up to see her, but Dad said no. She had been given only three months to live when she came out of hospital and as she was still alive now after five months, the doctors said it was her will to live to see me home, once more reunited with all my family. Therefore a sudden shock would not help her at all. He said he would go up first and break the news to her. I was indeed shattered completely. I could not believe that this could happen. I never gave a thought to anything like this occurring. It was unbelievable! My pure joy and elation on being back in the bosom of my family was now crushed into overwhelming sorrow! I was demented! Eileen asked me not to show too much emotion when I went upstairs and when my Dad called for me I just jumped about five stairs at a time.

Upon entering the bedroom I was taken aback, for laying there was just a frail person looking every bit like a 90 year old female. The shock was terrible, for as I said, I always pictured my Mother as I had left her some five years previous. The change was unfair and brutal. Another blow to my already damaged and scarred outlook on life and it's cruel ways. I conquered my sad feelings and held my dear Mother in my arms for an eternity of time. The joy our reunion inspired in her was there for all to see and through her illness came a very noticeable element of happiness. Her suffering pushed to one side and as best she could, she showed a Mother to Son feeling for the longing of so many years apart. It would be wrong of me to say that there were no tears shed. Tears of joy mixed with tears of sadness flowed from all of us who surrounded her bedside. I said I had sad memories with regards my Mum and it's painful, even now, to write these words for she was but 54 years of age at that time.

I remember talking to her for hour after hour until I noticed her eyes closing and I withdrew downstairs. I cried so much that evening. It had turned out to be a bitter sweet homecoming for I knew nothing of the illness which had struck my Mother down, yet I suppose it could have been worse had she not had that will and determination to hang onto life so we could be reunited. I do not think I would have been able to cope if she had been taken from me before I had a chance to shower her with my love in those last days of her life.

I recall, that night and many nights after, the great difficulty that I had in sleeping in a proper bed. I suppose also the fact that I had so much going through my mind did not help either.

I remember on one of my Mother's better days, Eileen and I put her in the wheel-chair, on to the train, and we journeyed up the coast to Southport, a sea side resort about 15 miles from Liverpool. We pushed her around and joked with her as much as possible. She appeared to enjoy it as much as we did. Trips like these were few and far between as her frail body could not stand too much movement. I had planned so many things to do with my Mum upon my return home. I often pictured walking around the village with her, linking arms and enjoying life as before. So much for plans!

Eric, next door, arrived home shortly after me. We had quite a reunion together, but sad thoughts for Stan and all our lost colleagues over in Europe, who never made it back. Eric, too, was upset over my Mum's illness. His homecoming helped me a lot for we would go out together in the afternoon as well as evenings and my mind was able to relax.

The local neighbours, knowing of my Mum's sickness, had made a point of arranging a Street Party for all the kids to celebrate The Homecoming of, what was to those kids, two Heroes! They would look at us as if we were something special, but we were not heroes. Just guys trying to survive a horrendous ordeal! Nice of those people though. I always admired them for all they did for me and my family in those early Post War days.

I recall my Brother, Jack coming home from school. A Boarding School in Surrey. He looked so big and was growing into a nice lad. I had heard many tales of things he did during local school days and of the many beatings he had got! Still, we all suffered at my Father's hand, and looking back it did us no harm. I heard my ex girl friend got married on the day after I arrived home. Needless to say, I did not get an invitation to the wedding! I did go to see her parents later as I always got on with them very well.

I spent many hours drinking and had a great reunion celebration with about six of us liberated POWs. That was some celebration! One lad came from Birmingham. One from Wales and from other English places. Jim Gomery was with us and we all finished up at his house. His Mum let us all sleep there, on the floor or wherever we laid our heads after a night of carousing.

I arranged a date with Madge and clearly recall her as a slim, petite beauty with long flowing hair. I remember her in a blue and white striped blouse, looking elegance itself! It wasn't long before we fell in love and we used to go around with Vi Evans and Eileen and end up in "The Hightown Pub" with a gang from the Sergeant's Mess in Blundellsands where we'd finish the night off.

Eileen's husband, Bill, was still away in the army and his eventual homecoming was another happy time for all. He became a great friend and pal of mine and we had some nice times which linger in my memory.

Things had altered since before The War. There was no "Bunny-Run." No more Dance Bands in the park. Things seemed different. Life had raced on six years and changes were there for all to see. Perhaps it was me! My Time Clock had stood still and now things were ganging up in my mind.

By the July of 1945 Madge and I became engaged. I proposed to her on a bench seat at Potters Bar and present day life was taking shape. Life was good. Freedom was wonderful and money was spent as if it was going out of fashion.

## Chapter 14
# Rehabilitation And Post War Life

After about ten weeks leave I was notified to report to a Rehabilitation Camp in Ilkley, West Yorkshire. The idea was to get you re-assimilated into civvie street once more. This was done by taking one out and about in groups, visiting factories, employment offices etc and discussing local requirements. In general, finding out the new set up in Post-War Britain.

If, upon a visit to a factory or work-shop, you considered you would like to take up employment there, then arrangements would be made with management for you to start as soon as you had completed the army course.

There were about six Liverpool lads at this centre and as soon as we found out just what they had in mind we asked for an interview, pointing out that, for us from the North-West to cover the area of West Yorkshire was a complete waste of time and we requested a transfer to a Camp adjacent to our home town.

Within a couple of days we were transfered to Peaover Hall near Knutsford, Cheshire. The set up there was much the same and besides, I met up with some of my Unit colleagues and was able to continue our comradeship. One in particular, was Frank McGauley who I am still great mates with to this day. We spent our time together both during the day and evenings as well, going for a drink and on occasions, going into Knutsford itself. Things were even better, as Frank had a motor bike! We used to go home at weekends. Returning to camp on the Monday morning.

It was decided that I should go into a Military Hospital for the long awaited skin graft on my arm that had been injured in the bombing at Piraeus Harbour. So, I ended up in Altringham, at a hospital that specialised in surgical grafts. Some of the patients there were in a dreadful state. Yet slowly but surely, their complete face or hands were reformed! A simply marvelous job was carried out on those unfortunate chaps. Albums were kept of the more serious cases and, as each graft was completed, so photos were taken and as you flipped through the pages you could see faces and hands slowly reemerging! There was always gaps between operations, which meant that some of the lads were in and out of hospital for a very long time. I saw fingers reconstructed not only with skin grafts, but also bone graft and it seemed that nothing was impossible for those amazing doctors!

My graft, I suppose, was a simple routine in comparison. I had to keep my arm up in a cage, suspended from above the bed for a lengthy period of time. Unfortunately I developed post operation pneumonia and was very ill for a few days. That passed and I used to look forward to the visits of Madge and Eileen at the weekends.

To get to the hospital they must have had to leave home about 7 or 8am in the morning, for they had to travel by bus, train and bus again to arrive at the hospital for visiting times. It certainly took some effort. Seeing them meant a lot to me and I wished the days away to bring the weekends quicker. It wasn't long before my graft had taken although they did warn me that possibly only half would take and then they would have to operate once more. A portion of the skin did in fact go black but it was around the edges though the doctors agreed that that area would heal on it's own. My leg too, where the German medics had taken the skin from to mend my arm, also healed so I was allowed to go home on a Friday till the Monday. Seeing my Mum was great, although her condition was slowly getting worse. But, just to hold her hand and know that, at least I was not too late, did compensate a little. Madge and I would spend a lot of time together and we arranged to get married on the 9th February 1946.

I was discharged from the hospital and returned to the Rehab Camp but didn't see anything that would have suited me employment wise. Besides, the area we covered was Manchester and that really didn't help Mersey siders. Even to this day people from Liverpool and Manchester, even only thirty miles away from each other, continue to remain arch rivals because of our fierce football team rivalry. To expect a Liverpudlian to even consider living or working in Manchester was just preposterous! I think we all finished there about the December of 1945 and returned home to await discharge.

That Christmas, which should have been a most wonderful day and happy time after such a long absence, was overshadowed by my dear Mother's deterioration. But still it was great to be with loved ones and know you were wanted. At least it was not a case of: Here goes another Christmas and another year around the corner with no hope of freedom and family. That was behind me. Now I had a future. A free man! A mind to call my own. It was heaven! I think I got myself drunk a lot at that time and well I might as I had a lot of socialising to catch up on! Five years and a youth to be exact!

1946 came, and so on the 10th January my darling Mother passed away. We were all at her bedside and believe me it was sadness itself. I broke my heart over that loss and I bitterly regretted that we only had a short time together on my release. WHY, has always been the question with me. Madge and I wanted to cancel our wedding as February seemed too close to this tragic event. But my Dad said, "No. Your Mother would not have wanted you to change this date."

We therefore were married on the 9th February 1946 at Saint Thomas of Canterbury Church, Great Georges Road, Waterloo.

Eric Hitchcock was my Best Man with Betty, Madge's sister, as the main bridesmaid. It was quite a wedding obviously, but we celebrated as best we could with our thoughts shooting back to our great loss. We went off to London for a honeymoon and the start of our married life together.

It was on the 6th February 1946 that I received my discharge papers from the army. I had joined the Territorial Army on the 28th March 1938 and my official discharge was 30th March 1946, showing my total service as eight years three days, with six years, two hundred and nineteen days war service—A lifetime in itself! My term of discharge was given as "Ceasing to fulfill army physical requirements" Meaning that I was 100% fit when I joined The Forces, but came out less than that. So endeth 2051895—Sapper/Lancashire/Corporal Gill's section of life that certainly produced a period not to be forgotten. I lost my rank upon discharge, as it was only a wartime promotion. At least that's what they said and I never bothered to challenge it. What the Hell!

I had no job when we got married. We had obtained a flat at 51 Handfield Road, Waterloo, where Eileen and Bill were living. It was a one bedroom with a kitchen and shared bathroom. We made great friends with the other tenants in the flats and shared some happy times together.

Eventually, I got a job at Cameron's Garage in Waterloo. It was due to Les Martin, Kenny Martin's Dad who worked there part-time in the petrol office. He spoke to Mr Cameron and that resulted in me starting as a semi-skilled worker. I had hoped to take a course in plumbing, but as the waiting list to commence the course was so long, I went to work in the garage instead. Bill Watson, upon his Army Discharge, also came to work at Cameron's and together we enjoyed our working days and, of course, our evenings out together. After a couple of years or so at the garage, I was getting fed up with indoor working and on going to one of our reunions, held in Liverpool, in which all the remaining members of "The Old Lancashire Fortress Royal Engineers" were present, I found myself in conversation with one of our Officers who was the Manager at the Scaffolding firm of "Big Ben" in Liverpool. He said "If you are fed up with working indoors than come along and I'll fix you up with a job."

Prior to that I had applied for the Ambulance Service which was just starting up under the new "National Health Service." Unfortunately I was not successful and so I went into the firm of scaffolding. Mr Cameron did not want me to leave. He even offered me more money to stay, but I wanted away.

I enjoyed the scaffolding work immensely. Plenty of variety. Plenty of travel. And, most of all, the money was good and they were giving bonuses in that firm even then.

Madge was working at Bootle Hospital in the sewing room. A part-time job, but it suited us. Due to my Dad living on his own and at his request, Madge and I went to live in Vermont Avenue. My Dad was working himself at this period, but shortly after we moved in he decided to retire. Everything was going well and we all got on well together.

After, almost four years of married life, Madge became pregnant. It was obvious that our relationship with my Dad was not going to continue as well as before with this new circumstance. There was only one living room in that house and, of course, my Father entertained his friends, who were all Seafarers and for us to need to stay in more to help in the social gatherings would not work. We would make a point of going out each time his mates came. Sometimes we would not feel like doing so, but we'd go because there was nowhere for us to put ourselves. It was time to feather our own nest.

I remember quite clearly the day our first born came into the world. It was a Sunday, the 20th August 1950 and I recall coming out of Church with my Dad and ringing Park House Nursing Home for news! To my delight they said "YES! your wife has had a daughter."

I dashed down on the bus and we both felt so proud and happy that after over four years of marriage, we had started a family. All those dark days of incarceration and despair were dispelled with the birth of new life. The 20th of August 1950 was indeed a date to remember. Our new and beautiful daughter, Patricia and Madge came home to my Dad's house but, after a short while, the atmosphere in the house was anything but good! So after yet another flare up with my Dad we decided to leave. We packed our little belongings into the pram and left Vermont Avenue. Plonking ourselves on Madge's Mum in her home in Parker Ave.

Now she was an easy going person and always had a house full with one or another of them. She had married a widower with twelve grown up children and had gone on to have six of her own, so she knew how to just take things in her stride! She made us welcome and we shared what space there was in her tiny house near to the banks of the River Mersey.

We used to have some smashing times. Going out altogether with one family member baby-sitting and taking turns while the others went out. The "Doric Pub" was a favourite place for us and we had some happy times with Doreen's husband, Jock, in that place. Doreen was Madge's sister and she had married a Scotsman from a small Scottish mining community called Pennicuik. Also John Prescot, Madge's step-brother, used to visit from his home over the water, on the other side of The Mersey River, and we would all, including Mother Prescot, end up in the pub.

As it really was overcrowded in Parker Avenue, we applied for a corporation house and were successful after some waiting time, when they built new property in Seaforth, a suburb of Liverpool, about ten miles west of the city centre. Our first real home together was at 14a Bower Grove. A flat, but it was nice.

Our number two daughter then came along. Again Madge went into Park House Nursing Home to have the baby.

It was a private medical facility, but nothing was too expensive to ensure the safe arrival of our long awaited babies. It was on 16th March 1952 that Helen was born. Our family was now four in number. I was so proud and really loved going out with my two lovely daughters and, of course, their lovely Mum as well. Because of our family increase we were allocated a

Pre-Fab home in De-Villiers Ave. These pre fabricated dwellings were invented, Post War, to house the many hundreds of thousands of people who were left homeless after five years of German Blitz bombings on our City and many other British towns. They were incredibly easy to assemble! Ready to be moved into within a day or two and they resembled square corrugated doll's houses.

To live in such a small home the designers had invented some ingenious storage ideas, For example. The kitchens were the fore runners of the "fitted" kitchens that we all have today. The pre fabs were cozy and warm and we were happy to live in this house for about three or four years.

It was a dream! Our first house and our own front door. Jack, my brother, had by this time decided to join the Navy. Eileen had a son called Robert and my Dad unfortunately had a slight stroke. This meant that my sister, Eileen, along with her family moved in to my Dad's house to look after him and, as Vermont Rd was too small a house for two families, which had been proved when Madge and I had lived there, they decided to buy a bigger property in Hasting Road, Waterloo. A bigger house and more rooms for all occupants to be able to enjoy some privacy in.

Bill was working on the Ribble Buses then as a Driver. Life was going along, but I'm sure we did not realise just how fast it was passing us by for our interests were many and our girls were of course our main and only concern.

# Chapter 15
# The Ambulance Service And How Our Life Progressed

I, by this time, was a member of the Ambulance Service, Helen. Having joined in August 1951. The 20th to be exact. It was one evening when Madge spotted the advert in the Liverpool Echo and said "There is that job again that you applied for in 1948. You need to check it out again."

I reluctantly sent off for details because I enjoyed the scaffolding job a lot. I got a reply, an interview, medical and driving test all on the same day and also a starting date. Even then I felt I didn't want to leave my job as as scaffolder. The money was good. The work interesting and traveling around suited me fine. But,I realised that scaffolding was a short career, for even over 40 year olds were often restricted to ground work and not long after that they found themselves out of work altogether. So, after a lot of thought and agonising about the future I went into The Service, knowing that the wages were far, far below what I'd been getting at Big Ben. £5 per week to be exact. In 1954 that converted to about $12 per week!

We now had a third little daughter, Lorraine. Born 2nd April 1953, This time the baby was born at home, in the Pre-Fab in De-Villiers. Another beauty, and my heart was full of joy. Money was not as free then. Besides Madge did not want to leave the other two girls with someone else and so she stayed at home to look after our brood. Eileen did help out at that time and we were most grateful for that. We now had a house full of females. Plus one male and I learned later that that was indeed a draw back, to say the least!

My recollections of those early family days were of happiness and joy. Pride and perfection. Of life meaning more than at any time I had imagined possible, especially during those dark days of the early 1940's when I had no future, no hope and no liberty!

It was hard work, especially for Madge, with all the washing, feeding and looking after us all, but she managed marvelously and was the perfect Mum.

Money, as I said, was not great, but as I had been granted a disability pension for my war wounds, we didn't do too bad. How I have wished for that period of my life to return! What a pity we cannot turn the clock back and keep it at what suits you best .

Jack had his 21st Birthday in 1954. I was unable to attend the party as I had contracted jaundice and was off work for a period of five weeks. The function was held at The Queen's Hotel in Waterloo, and everyone had a good time. At least, that's what they told me!

Later Eileen and Bill emigrated to Canada, Bill traveling first. They had difficulties with my Dad and things did not work out so he was left on his own, having retired from his work back in 1947/48. He was never an easy man to live with, even my beloved Mother would have admitted that.

We moved from the Pre Fab to a brick construction, on the same estate. Number 8, Barncroft Place. It was a nice three bedroomed, spacious house, but, unfortunately, in the wrong place as was to be proved later. My job in the Ambulance Service was going well. I enjoyed the work and can, even now, recall the very first case that I went out on.

I had not been on the Station more than half an hour when they got an Emergency Call to South Road. There was only one other chap on the station available, so they sent me out with him. I hadn't a clue about First-Aid or any sort of aid! But, off we went. It turned out to be a woman shopper whose shopping bag had caught in the front wheel of her bike and, off she came, splitting her chin open. Fortunately for me, she had been taken into a chemist shop close by and they had given her lint to cover the wound. The site of this injury was very difficult to bandage, so we took her to Waterloo Hospital where they put a couple of stitches in. I can still picture that lady even now and although I have not seen her around for many years, I used to, for long enough, recall many details of her appearance. I recall she had ginger hair and that "Ginger look" just like those sort of people do!

Before Bill went to Canada, he too worked in the Ambulance Service. A vacancy came up and I told him to apply. He was successful in his application and was accepted. When in uniform, he and I looked very similar and on many occasions we were mistaken for one another! Many times patients would say "You brought me into hospital this morning!"

When, in fact, it was not me who had transported them. It was Bill, my brother in Law! I remember one time when Bill was on leave, I thought "I'll grow a mustache. That should stop the confusion!"

Upon Bill's return to work he walked in sporting a mustache! Blimey! That was a joke believe me! What a coincidence! You see how we shared quite a lot of life together and because of that we were always very close. He was good company and never stuck for conversation!

I recall one Christmas when we were all up at Vermont Ave for the day, we realised we had run out of milk, so Bill and I agreed we would go round to Handfield Rd, to their flat and bring some back. We collected the milk and then decided we would just call into The Liver Pub for a quick drink. As we came out Bill dropped the bag and, Bingo, the milk was gone. Smashed to smithereens! That took some explaining to the waiting families.

At the Ambulance Service, I worked for almost eight years on Day-Work, due to the fact that each time a vacancy came up for a position on shift work, they would transfer one of the staff from the Formby station, as that site was in the process of closing down. During those 8 years I worked, first, with Millie Prescott, a female who had been in the Service during the war, then, George Reed, who was on the same interview as me, but did not start till a later date because he had to have his teeth pulled out and a false set fitted. We teamed up together.

Then they opened a new station at Maghull. They asked for volunteers from Crosby and Burscough to man the full 24 hour station. I did not fancy traveling all that way to Maghull, about 15 miles, as I only had a bike and if the weather was bad it would mean out early for a bus and that would mean more money. So I decided to remain where I was in Crosby and near to home. It turned out that they did not get enough volunteers so, George Reed and Bill Watson, as they were last in, were detailed to go to Maghull.

When they had left I was paired up with a chap, name of Jimmy Budd. He was also a good mate and we had many laughs together. He was older than I and did not drive as when he came into The Service in 1949, they were only employed as attendants, but that policy did not work out and some had driving licenses so they were OK. Jimmy could not drive and did not want to so I was able to do all the driving necessary. Unfortunately, he died about 1960, after being off work with heart trouble. It appeared to clear up and he was due to return to work when, over the Christmas period, he collapsed and died. Sad, and a good friend gone.

I soon was voted into taking over the Station Workers' Union. "The National Union of Public Employees". I was mainly the instigator in forcing The Union to form a separate Ambulance Branch, instead of having us mixed with hospital workers and other Council employees. The reason I wanted to have the Ambulance branch separate was because, at the regular Branch meetings there was always so much business for them to sort out that we never got a chance to bring our points up. I then found myself elected to the position of Branch-Secretary, followed by election onto the Ambulancemans Whitley Council Committee with meetings down in London. I was also voted onto The Union Advisory Committee, which involved further meetings in London. I enjoyed union work, and enjoyed helping other colleagues with problems which I could help solve. I was a moderate in my stance and accepted therefore by management.

Family life was going on and the girls growing up. Attending school and becoming very interesting. We all went to Butlins Holiday Camp at Pwllheli, North Wales. It was our first holiday as a family and we all enjoyed it immensely. Butlins was a huge army camp looking resort. The camp had hundreds of tiny chalets where families stayed for a week or so. All the entertainment, dining rooms and sports were on site and included in the cost. There was also supervised play groups for the children to get involved in and it gave them a chance to meet other young children. One thing that always stays in the minds of the girls was the amazing indoor swimming pool. When you were in the restaurant area you could see people swimming through a series of windows that were built below the water level of the elevated swimming pool. The girls would spend ages just watching the antics of all the swimmers. Usually, just their legs flaying around or a couple of divers swimming under to the windows to look out at the diners. The children found plenty to do and Madge and I were able to get around on our own knowing the girls were well looked after.

Before the children were born, Madge and I went over to Ireland, up to Scotland, also to The Isle of Man. We enjoyed all those trips and met some very nice people, but Butlins was something special and I'm sure we all remember it well.

Eventually, I went onto shift work at Crosby Station and was soon a Leading Ambulanceman. I used to relieve as Station Office when the occasion arose. My mate then was Bill Kinrade, a really great fellow and not only a workmate but a friend. We had an excellent working relationship and it was a pleasure to go to work. He was a typical Scouser with the wonderful sharp wit and eternal optimism that Liverpool people have in abundance. He also became involved in union work and was the Branch Chairman, as I was the Secretary. Yes, a good mate and a great friend.

The 1960's were a wonderful era for Liverpool Football Club and I was, and still am, an ardent supporter of this popular British sport. I loved the club and still do, I recall most of all season 1964/65 when I was at Wembley Stadium to see Liverpool win the F-A Cup for the very first time, beating the then old rivals, Leeds, by 2 goals to 1, after extra time. What a thrill! And my first ever trip to Wembley, the home of our English football games based in London. I went alone but paled up with a chap from Aintree. We had a ball! Especially after the game! Celebrations galore! Ian St John scored the winner after Rodger Hunt had equalised. Many fine games were played and won in that period and many fine players were members of the club.

As a family, our next holiday was down around Somerset and North Devon by car. Staying at different Bed and Breakfast houses en-route. That was all great! It was a hire car and the cost of this holiday came from one of the many part time jobs that I did for extra cash. Madge, too worked as a part-time waitress at The Blundellsands Hotel in Crosby. So, between us, we managed to purchase a car. A second-hand Austin A40. We had some good trips in that and it got us out and about more.

Around that period I recall agreeing to Madge going on holiday with her friend, Sally Feely. They decided to go to Spain and I was all in favour for Madge had worked very hard bringing up the girls. She never complained and I considered it was about time she had a complete break. I took time off work and looked after the family. Why, even now, they still recall some of the lovely meals that I created for them. Right Helen! One, in particular. I decided to be a little adventurous and try out a new and popular dish called a curry. I had bought all the ingredients, as well as the small tin of curry powder. As I wasn't a very experienced chef nor did I know how little powder you needed to make the meal hot and spicy, I just used the whole tin! The girls took one mouthful and grimaced. So much for trying out new recipes!

We had all gone to Liverpool Airport to see Madge and Sally off and upon their return, we decorated the living room with Welcome-Home-Banners. Everyone got involved. That was fun! We had missed her a lot and were really glad when the two weeks were over and she was back with us. I think the girls were relieved as there would be no more opportunities to use them as guinea pigs for my new culinary skills!

As I was now on Shift-Work, it became more and more difficult for me to get sleep when I was on night shifts as the house was next to a playing field and our outer wall was used for a goal during the winter and as a cricket wicket in the summer making it impossible to relax and sleep in the daytime. So, in the end, I decided to sell the car and go in for a house of our own. The Corporation would not consider a transfer for us so there was no alternative. We would have to purchase our own property. These Corporations have always been a law on to themselves. If your face fits you are alright. That sort of policy annoys me immensely and, if I had my way, I'd kick the lot out. No bother!

We were successful in finding a nice house at number 9 Vogan Ave. Here, I was in my late forties starting out with Mortgage Payments! It was good, however, as the girls were growing up and it was better they too had a brighter outlook and environment.

Growing up brought many problems to the family, for at this stage, the girls started to think for themselves. They no longer wanted to be told what to do and what not to do. This part of my life became something of a nightmare for I knew what pitfalls there were in life. I knew what my sex were like as regards females and I considered that it was my duty as a Father to guide the children through those difficult and vulnerable  years no matter what the outcome cost and it did cost me a lot but I had to do it, alone and like the song sung by a favourite crooner of Madges, Frank Sinatra, sang. "I DID IT MY WAY!" AND FOR THAT I HAVE NO REGRETS! I know the girls too must have played their part, but as a parent one can only see the worst and must protect, at all costs, despite the brickbats or the unpleasantness that accompanies this stance.

School days had ended for Patricia. She got a job with The Blackburn Insurance Company in Liverpool City centre. I took her down to Liverpool on her first day. I felt so sorry for her, starting out on this new phase of her life as I could recall just how she must have felt.

Lorraine and you, Helen were at Seafield Convent Grammar School, both having won academic scholarships from Saints Peter and Pauls Junior School. The three girls did well at school and also had little part-time jobs to help provide better standards for themselves and earn a little cash for themselves to spend. Soon both Helen and Lorraine left school. Life was speeding on. I continued to enjoy my job but there were many sad moments involved. None worse than the Emergency Call that I was sent out to deal with on 23rd December 1957.

It was to number 13 Hastings Road, Waterloo. The home of my Father. From the information given to us ambulance crew, it appeared that it was a collapse and nothing more serious than that. When I arrived and fearing the worst, I rushed up the stairs to find my Dad laying on the floor of the bathroom and he was dead. What a shock! And how much it did upset me. Taking my own Father to Waterloo Hospital for Death Certification was a desperately sad affair for me. As my colleague at the time did not drive I had to drive my own Father's body to the local hospital. I knew, only too well, that my Dad's end had happened and when the Station were informed, they sent over another driver and then took me home. How heartbreaking it is to lose your second parent. I felt so sorry and sad. That Christmas I spent with my dear Dad's body in his home in Hasting Road. That was the least I could do to show my respect, for he had many good and sincere ways.

He was a hard man who had lead his life in the way he thought best and he, with my Mum, was responsible for our being on this earth. For that alone we owed them much. My Dad lead a lonely life without his partner, just as many do. I felt he was waiting to die, and at least he did not suffer too much, although inwardly, no one would know what turmoil he went through. Only he would know. So endeth my contact with my parents. I was now without the fact of having them around. Everyone goes through this life stage and the sadness lingers all one's life. But life must go on and in my case the passing of my dear Father under those tragic circumstances did give me, in my job, much more sympathy and feeling for the people who also suffered the same tragic events.

The Ambulance Service, to me, was a wonderful job to be in. People really showed their appreciation for the attendance and care of an Ambulance Crew, especially during late evening and early morning hours. So many problems seem to happen during those times and you are not only a First-Aider on such occasions, but also a diplomat, a person to confide in, a go-between and in many cases, a Saviour! You need to adapt to upper class and working class patients. You need the skills of a Social Worker and knowledge of a Medical Man! You get praise. You get abuse, but most of all, you get satisfaction from everything you do and every case that comes your way. One is dedicated and unless your heart and soul are in the job, then you are better out of it for you damage the image of the organisation. I never regretted my move into the Service, although at first I was a bit apprehensive.

A chance remark made by Harry Carson, the then Station Officer at Crosby, completely changed my position with the Lancashire Ambulance Service. He mentioned to me, during one of our discussions "Do you know that you have sacrificed promotion for "The Union" in this service?"

At first I thought nothing of this comment, but upon reflection, I thought "Well here I am a Leading Ambulanceman and also covering for the Station Officer Post during sickness and leave. Is it possible that because of my Union activities I would be held back? Should I try for a Station of my own to control?"

This, I decided, was something I needed to find out for myself. Although vacancies were few and far between on Management level, it so happened that one came available at Billinge Station. So I duly applied and awaited the outcome.

Eventually I was short listed and went with six other chaps for interview at Wigan Health Offices. It was a full Health Committee Board, about twelve people around the table in the Board-Room. Well the seven applicants were reduced to four, I being one of the candidates who had been short listed. So far so good! After a second session of questioning the chap who had been doing the Stand-In at the Station, due to the ill health of the Station Officer, was successful and rightly so, he landed the post. I considered that I did fairly well for my first attempt and my fears of my Union involvement being used against me seemed to be unfounded. I worked on at Crosby Station quite happily and with a good mate, Bill Kinrade.

There were, at times, some distressing cases to deal with, especially on the occasions when one would get a call out to a child accident and when you arrived you'd find a little toddler underneath an Ice-Cream Van or something similar. I had two such cases during my period at Crosby and recall one small boy, as we put him on the slab in the Mortuary. The threepenny piece he had been clutching when he was racing to buy his ice cream, fell from his hand. Sad indeed and the memory lives with you for quite some time as you can see.

In early 1972 there was a new Station built at Skelmersdale. A twelve vehicle bay, and one of the biggest and most up to date in the county. One Ambulance and one Dual-Purpose Vehicle had been operating from an old factory for about eighteen months. This system had sufficed up until this time as Skelmersdale was a new town, just being built. George Cosgrove was in charge there as Leading Ambulanceman. A temporary position until the new station was ready. The position for Officer-in-Charge at the new station had to be advertised within The Service and I duly applied. Once more, I was shortlisted as were five others, including George, who according to all, was firm favourite to get the job.

When my turn came to get interviewed I was grilled for quite a period about my Union position, stance etc, but as it turned out my answers seemed to impress them. I think it helped too that, as they mentioned, I had been only a Moderate in my Union approach and also that I had helped, not only my fellow workers but also Management in avoiding serious conflicts between Management and workers.

Furthermore I used my Union work to point out to them that I had an added advantage over the other applicants in as much that I knew how to solve any problems that may arise from both sides. My approach to this interview was one of; Well, if I get the job, all well and good and if I don't I, at least proved my point. Besides I liked working at the Crosby Station. Further Harry Carson, my Station Officer at Crosby, had said when I was going up to Ormskirk for the interview "I wish you luck, but I hope you don't get the job as I consider your presence on this station has always been an asset to everyone and I, for one, do not want to lose you"

Mind you, he and I had many arguments over work related issues and his treatment of staff at various times. Still nice of him to say what he did. It showed that he had respect for me and I can assure you that I rated him highly as an Officer on my list.

To almost everyone it was considered quite a shock that I was appointed for the job and not George. But later I learned that, in the opinion of the interviewing panel there was only one person for the job and that, of course, was me! George was more then disappointed. He was offered a return to the Maghull Station or to stay at Skelmersdale working under my guidance. He chose to stay and I, for one was pleased as we had always been good mates and friends throughout our working lives. He too had worked at Crosby in the early days and on and off we worked together, but when Maghull opened he transferred over there as he only lived a short distance from the station.

So in June 1972 I became a Rank Seven Station Officer in charge of a brand new, large station. It was not long before I became Rank Six and it also was not too long, just two years after Skelmersdale opened, that Tommy Owen, the Officer in Charge at the Burscough Station applied and was successful in obtaining a post as Instructor at the Ambulance Training School, so creating an Officer vacancy at Burscough. George Cosgrove applied and this time I more or less forced him to approach the interview in a stronger and more determined manner. He took my advice and was accepted and his appointment was the start of a really great working relationship between him and I. It was second to none. We shared any problems that arose at either station. We would continually discuss everything appertaining to the running and well-being of The Service in the Ormskirk area. The bosses from Headquarters were hardly ever seen in our patch. It was an accepted thing that George Cosgrove and Frank Gill were more than capable of running the Ambulance Service successfully without interference or guidance from higher levels.

Everything was going well, but I did miss the real Ambulance work, like being on shifts and dealing with the problems of the public and putting my skills to the use that I had been trained for. Still, it was my choice and here I was deep into Management. Courses were many. I enjoyed them all! I decided I would have a try at the Institute of Ambulance Personnel Course. A private venture and one spanning out over about thirteen weeks. Two visits per week at the St Helen's Technical College. Eight different subjects: Central Government, Local Government, Road Traffic Laws, Stores, Stores Accounting, Health Service Act and two stages of Management. The final two days of exams took place at The Liverpool Ambulance Service Training School. Four papers each day and a pass grade was required in all eight subjects. The whole course seemed very difficult indeed and as most of the class were much younger than myself, I did not think I would stick the distance. But, I attended every week and studied each subject as best I could during the remaining days of each week.

We had to wait ages for the results and I recall that each of us had a number only which was allocated to us at the exam. One morning, when I just got into work, I had a phone call from a chap who had sat the exam with me. He had just received his results through the post and he had remembered my number and surprised me by informing me that I'd passed! I didn't really accept this information until I arrived home myself that evening and checked my own mail.

It was true! Only around five or six out of about twenty who attended the Liverpool exam had been successful. I was thrilled and happy! As I said, all the other chaps were years younger than I! Must have been my lucky period. I eventually had my Diploma presented to me at a Health Committee Meeting in Preston and felt very proud on that occasion. By this time I was 54/55 years of age and at last I could afford a new car. My very first new one! I was really chuffed. It was great. Nowadays a new car comes easy to younger people and I don't suppose they appreciate it as I did. But this was my life.

The Girls were still growing up fast. Patricia had her 21st Birthday celebration. We organised a party at home, attended by quite a big crowd. You Helen, were married. Too young I thought, although I must admit I often wished, had I had the opportunity, I would like to have been married sooner than I was. But then I'm not sure which works best! Lorraine, too, was due to be married and our family was slowly breaking up as you each went your own separate ways. Another mile stone in my life.

A big feature in my working career was the fact that I could not bear to see an injustice done to any of my fellow work-mates. I think perhaps this was due to my being trodden down for so long as a POW and unable to react or retaliate in any manner of finding a solution. Anyway, I had served my colleagues when I was involved in Union activities while a member of the ambulance road staff. Now, upon my promotion, I resigned from my London Committee and also from my Branch Secretary's post. Much to the annoyance of the Union Officials, who in fact were under the impression that I had been forced to give up my Union activities upon my promotion to Station Officer. This was not the case at all! I thought that, for my own good, it would be better to pack in as if something cropped up that did not suit the members, they would in all probably point the finger and say. "He's not as efficient as he used to be before promotion!"

So I quit. I was presented with a lovely clock for the work I had done and I am very proud of that. Besides, there are many instances within the Ambulance Service of the good work that I did and I'm also proud of those memories.

I still kept on my Union Membership and it was not long before I found myself Chairman of the Station Officers Union Branch. Also, I was the negotiator with the Station Officer from Burnley, Gerry Foulds, on all local matters concerning Officers. Between us we were successful in having Officer coverage within Lancashire for Bank-Holidays. Payment of Home Phones. Payment of regular overtime during leave. To list just a few.

I was also elected on to the Shop Stewards Committee for Management. Onto the Equipment Committee and also Welfare Committee. With this latter Committee I helped to form a Death Grant Organisation to give help to Widows or Husbands of any Ambulance Member within Lancashire who died prematurely. This amendment will continue for as long as members go on subscribing to this programme.

As you can see I was deeply involved with the running of The Service and I was very familiar with all aspects of the organisation. Thus I thought it was about time to pursue further promotion within Lancashire.

## Chapter 16
# Promotion Failure
# And My Farewell To The
# Ambulance Service

I had been asked to apply for the Blackpool Station post upon the retirement of their present Station Officer. This station was a fifty-man-staff and it covered a very large area. But, for home reasons, I did not take up the challenge.

We had not long moved into a Bungalow and another upheaval was not too keenly acceptable.

Eventually, a vacancy came up for an Assistant Divisional Officer for South Ribble and I duly applied. I was convinced beyond doubt, that I could handle that position adequately. This was also the opinion of many at Headquarters and most of the road staff. There were five for interview, including outsiders from other Authorities. I was satisfied with my efforts at the interview, but alas I was not successful and I regret that failure, as that would have been the highlight of my career. The pinnacle for me and all the hard work that I had put into the Ambulance Service.

I knew then, just how George Cosgrove must have felt upon my appointment at the Skelmersdale Station. Still, thats life. We don't always get everything we want! You just look back with disappointment.

I carried on with my job and enjoyed doing it. The years were flying by, and I mean flying! Eileen had been over from Canada a couple of times on holiday. Her marriage to Bill Watson had, unfortunately ended in a bitter divorce and she had gone on to make a wonderful and fun single life for herself over in Canada. It was always great to see her. Although she does YAP-A-Lot!

I, with Jack, my younger brother, had always been very close and I think it is right that family members should stay close, for when the parents have gone, the link, if there, between brothers and sisters keeps alive the memories of growing up, of family life and joys spent when young. Also the relationship, when you reach adulthood, is important, for where can you find a better person to associate with then your own!

I had found this with Jack. We both enjoyed football and had shared many exciting times together watching Liverpool Football team. Also, we enjoyed our regular Friday evenings out and looked forward to them coming around each week. We always had plenty to talk about and many laughs. Remember, he too was part of my Mum and Dad, so why shouldn't I enjoy his company as I do Eileens. Mind you, I did fall out with Jack before my Dad died. That was mostly caused by his wife and also, the fact that when he came home on shore leave from the Navy, he did not always go and see his Dad. That part to me was wrong.

1977 saw Madge and I off to Canada for the first time. We went with George and Muriel Cosgrove and a couple of their friends, Dot and Sid. It was a great trip and a memorable one. Even though we stayed with our own relatives we used to meet up while there and shared many happy times although Eileen's second marriage was not good.

It was a real shock when she and Bill broke up, for Bill was, to us, a grand chap and they always seemed suited. Her second husband, Art and her were only married a short time before problems began to arise and they too were divorced. Guess it's the way things were out in Canada at the time.

1980 saw Tricia married to a guy from Dublin who she had met whilst she was living and working in London. How I recall that evening back here in the Bungalow. Gosh those Irish! Or, at least, some of them! They are real nuts to say the least! It was great fun and everyone had a smashing time.

Your marriage, Helen, had ended. That was a sad period for us all. We thought everything was working out well, but how wrong we were! Parents feel very strongly when things do not work out but we cannot alter the downfalls of life and we have to accept them as they come.

We were to suffer a further blow when Lorraine's marriage also broke up. Another sad event and one which we shared with sorrow and concern. Fortunately, in both cases there were no children to complicate the situations. All this you know about but since I started this encyclopedia I have found myself just rabbiting on at times and bringing my life up to date. On reflection there are a number of things which I have not mentioned but are deep in my memory and have formed part of my rather dull life.

For instance, I well remember the one and only time that my Dad took us camping. This was in North Wales. We camped in a field and, as I recall, my Mum would not sleep in the tent at all! She slept in the car. The weather was not good so I don't think we stayed there long, but more than anything I recall the lovely ham and eggs we had in the Farm House each morning. The ham was hanging up to cure from the ceiling and slices were cut from it there and then. Delicious!

I see, quite clearly the trips that Madge and I used to take over to New Brighton and enjoy long walks along the promenade. We would travel on the Overhead Railway in Liverpool to The Pier Head and get the Ferry across The Mersey. It still steams back and forth across our famous River even to this day. Gosh! Happy times. The same Overhead Railway, years later, that I used to take the girls on to see all the ships in the Docks, right along the water-front. Gee how things have changed. Not for the better believe me!

What about all the stories I used to cook up about the Elephant and the little girl at the circus! You girls would jump onto our bed on a weekend morning and plead for another installment of Jumbo and the buns. The story told amid great silence and joy. You were spellbound! Why did those wonderful days have to end?

Oh yes, I remember on the trip out to Egypt on the HMS Cape Town Castle when we were billeted in the cabins. Four to each berth. I was in charge of our accommodation and beer was strictly forbidden. Well, card schools were regular and one evening with extra lads in playing cards, one of them knocked a full bottle of beer down from the top bunk and, Bang! It went right through the wash basin. As the NCO in Charge,I had to go before the Commanding Officer to explain the cause of the "accident". I remember saying that a hair brush fell so causing the damage. After a long silence and some consultation the CO said. "If you say it was a hair brush Corporal, then it must have been a  hair brush. Case Dismissed!"

I don't think he ever really believed me but it was the best I could come up with for, as I said, beer was not allowed in the cabins.

Another incident during my army days occurred when at Perch Rock Battery in New Brighton. Stan Field was on Guard and I went out to talk to him. Out of the dusk walked the Artillery Officer in charge of the Battery. I immediately said, without being asked "I was only telling him the time!"

The immediate reaction of the Officer was to reply. "He who excuses, accuses!"

This saying stuck deep in my memory and was used by me on many occasions especially as an Ambulance Officer.

During my time of employment on the Scaffolding, I was working in a church outside Warrington and during our dinner break, while walking around the very old grave yard, reading the inscriptions on the Memorial Stones, one really stood out to me. It read:

"AS YOU ARE NOW SO, ONCE WAS I!
AS I AM NOW SO YOU WILL BE!
SO, BE PREPARED TO FOLLOW ME!"

How true that adage is of all stages of life! As I grew older many colleagues at work would say "You old So and So!" or "You're too old." or "You are getting old!"

Well I used to quote to them----

"AS YOU ARE NOW SO ONCE WAS I
AS I AM NOW SO YOU WILL BE!"

I was noted for making this remark. It became my trademark phrase, but it is so apt.

I made many friends within all the Ambulance Authorities. I was more than well known throughout Merseyside and also Lancashire districts. I always spoke my mind and was never afraid to speak out if I thought it was necessary.

I remember at one full Officer Meeting held at Broughton, one of the Senior Officers was slating all the road staff something ridiculous. Everyone sat and listened until I, for one, could stand no more, so I said "Say what you like about staff, but exclude Skelmersdale for such events do not take place there."

His reply was "It's alright, Mr Gill. We all know about you and your staff at Skelmersdale." To which I responded "Well, that's OK by me as long as you don't forget it!"

I was not over popular with that man from that time. He was a Southerner and left Lancashire after a spell. Not to be missed I can assure you.

Then came 1982. In that year I did my first Parachute jump which wasn't too successful. I was 63 years old. You, Helen, had done one down at Peterborough, at a private parachute Instruction School and I thought it looked great and wanted to have a go myself.

I booked in at Burscough Parachute Club, did the training and waited for the weather to be right. You were with me Helen. but no luck that weekend. The wind was too strong and unfortunately you had to return to London. So, after a few weekends attending and waiting for the perfect breeze, at last we went up 2,500 feet and bang, I made my first fixed line parachute jump from a light aircraft. All went well until, on the last fifty or so feet, I pulled one of my guide cords instead of the two at the same time, and so drifted off course and came down with terrible thud! I hurt my back but I suppose was lucky not to break a limb. I suffered a lot of pain and it was months and months before it all cleared up. A few years later I was stricken with agonising back pain and, on further medical investigation, it was discovered that I had a hairline fracture of my spine! It took all those years for the injury to take it's toll. After being laid up for a number of weeks I was able to fully recover from this potentially devastating injury.

At this time too I remember you went off to teach in Bogota, Columbia, South America. You had definitely inherited my father's traveling bug and off you went to work and explore this great continent. I know when you were there it was difficult to keep in touch as there were no computers to link people where ever they were based. So we had to rely on letters and occasional long distance phone calls. You had a wonderful time over there and managed to explore extensively. You have told me since returning that that was the time you decided you needed to encourage me to commit my life experiences to paper.

Despite this, I was still keen to prove to myself that I could drop out of the sky correctly and more importantly land properly. When you, Helen, arranged a further jump in Devon with the Royal Navy Royal Marines, I was delighted to get my second chance to prove I could be successful. Again, after training, the weather was not conducive for parachuting and another trip had to be arranged. So it was, on the 3rd December 1983, I floated down correctly and really enjoyed the whole setup. That was because you Helen shared that event with me! Many experiences that you enjoyed, you always wanted to include me in.

Remember, we jumped again on the Sunday morning and Boy, it was lovely! Do you recall that you used the parachute that I had packed the night before? It was the policy that, after the students had jumped, they had to collect their canvas and take it back to the hanger and, under supervision, repack the chute. When it was your turn to choose a chute the Instructor asked if you wanted to use the chute that your dad had repacked. What could you say? Well, I worried about that quite a bit but, Thank God, it deployed as expected and you landed safe and sound.

All the lads there were great and we had a smashing time all round. Our first night there we went down to the local village, Dunkeswell, for a couple of drinks and ended up staying for a disco! When we drove back to the airfield a real "Pea Souper" of a fog had descended onto the whole airfield. I remember, quite vividly, how we were driving on the airfield road, trying to get our bearings and locate the billet where we were staying. After a number of cautious minutes we realised that we were driving up THE RUNWAY !!! We laughed so much about that, even though we would have been in serious trouble if we had been discovered .

1983 proved an eventful year for I decided to take an early retirement from the Ambulance Service. The main reason was the fact that it used to bug me to think that if I was unfortunate enough to "snuff it" before reaching 65 then a large part of my Retirement Lump Sum would be lost and Madge would only get a percentage of it. It was a decision that was very difficult to make and difficult to come to terms with for I loved my job and every aspect of it was a joy. Still, I would have to finish sometime so why not twelve months early? When I did submit my request the Authority asked me to stay a short while longer. So July 1983 it was, although with leave etc, my final day was late September 1983.

On my last day at work the lads had decked out an Ambulance with a big white sheet with kind words written upon it. While sharing a laugh or two about this, up rolled the Assistant Chief Officer, Peter Wilkinson! It was then only 8:15am, He had left his home in Preston around 7:30am as he had to go to Manchester for a meeting and he did not want the day to pass without he wished me a long and happy retirement. Later in the day the Chief Officer also arrived with the same message. All very nice, but rather upsetting, but really shows that you were appreciated for the job that was entrusted to you. Towards the end of September a marvelous retirement party was arranged for me at Upholland Hall by Cyril Walker, a member of the fine staff that I had. It was a full house! So many friends turned up and most of all my whole family were present. All three of you girls. Helen had just returned from her travels in the jungles of South America. Also Eileen and Jack. It was a proud moment! Also a complete evening for me having everyone there to share the event and to see and hear some very appreciative words spoken by Mr Jones, the Chief Officer. Many gifts were presented to me on that night and I never realised till then just how much friendship meant to so many. As a matter of fact, I felt very embarrassed receiving all those gifts and was glad when that part of the evening ended.

It was indeed more than a problem for me to get used to finishing work. I also missed all my working friends and patients. The routine of every day. The coming and going to work. The fact of getting up each morning to leave home and attend to the needs of providing a service for sick people who rely so much on the Ambulance Service. Supervising my staff. To see to their needs. To know that they needed you as much as you needed them. Their welfare was so important in my book of rules and I was happy doing my job of Station Officer, but it all ended and I was now a "Has Been!"

I became a person reaching the twilight of life. The sunset of working life had caught up with me. I had joined the many awaiting the final ride, feeling that there were many, many things I had not done and wanting to relive many parts of my life that had been good. I had a  desire to, see again, people who had played a part in my life. Such things do not enter one's mind when working but as soon as you are idle you reminisce a lot. Probably too much! Having time on your hands is not really good for it's alright to say relax, but relaxation forces the mind into thought and thoughts go back and back where you picture events as they were, when in fact they don't allow for time. It's difficult to explain and much more difficult to understand. I don't know if it happens to everyone the same but I know how retirement has effected me. They say that one's life is planned from the time of birth till you reach the end. Well, if that's so, then I don't think a lot of my planner.

Yet, during my life I have experienced; Excitement, Fear, Pain, Depression, Disappointment, Upset, Sadness, Heartbreak, Joy, Laughter, Love, Understanding, Respect, Friendship, Health, Employment. What more can one want from life?

I suppose I have had my fair share of the events to be expected from life. I've always had my share of financial benefits. I've enjoyed a fair standard of living, worked hard for what I've got and will leave this life with a lot more than when

I came into it. 80 perhaps! I'm being a little too deceptive when I blame my planner. At least I have been given three score plus years to achieve the position I hold this day. I can come and go as I please. I can hold my head up very high and for this I thank my parents. I have Madge to share life with and, all in all, I'm sure there are many who would change places with me at any-time.

## Chapter 17
# After Thoughts And Conclusion

I enjoyed the Gliding event, Helen, that you arranged with a teaching colleague of yours from London, Phil Turner. It was quite an experience!

I enjoyed the flying lessons that Madge arranged for a birthday present for me. That too was something special. The Scuba-Diving was another event that was new to me but something different and something I would never have done without you Helen. I have enjoyed the holidays we've had, but I must admit that when on holiday in Norway I had a very unpleasant flash back to my dark, war time prisoner days.

We had sailed up one of the long Fjords, to a hotel in the middle of no where. The ferry we arrived on was the only way in and the only way out of that area and the ferry operated just once a week! That did, indeed, upset me a great deal. I felt trapped! I felt as if I was again a POW and my inward feelings were tumultuous and indescribable! I was glad to leave that place for I WAS upset believe me!

Again, while on holiday in Yugoslavia, I overheard some of the German holiday makers with that German accent which reminded me of periods of my years in confinement. That was also upsetting and no one will know or even understand the effect that such matters have upon me! It stirs up deep seated wounds and turns joy to dismay. Fortunately incidents like those don't last long and I enjoy foreign visits. I would like to do a lot more but who knows.

What now does the future hold for me. Well mostly I would like to see both you Helen and you Lorraine married and settled like Patricia. It's important to share your life with someone and have a home and interests enjoyed by discussion, love and understanding. I would like to live long enough to see little Holly pass baby stage, pass early childhood and understand just what a Grand-Dad is all about.

What a wonderful day the 2nd November 1984 was!
Our first Grand-Child! A really lovely, darling little girl.
As I say, I hope we can enjoy her.

As I bring this letter up to date, let me just put into writing
some of the sayings that my dear Father passed on to me when
I was starting out in life. I remember them clearly and can say,
without fear of contradiction that they were indeed wise words

"Make all the friends you can for your
enemies will be made for you."
ABSOLUTELY TRUE!-

"Trust no one any-time and you'll be right sometime."
ABSOLUTELY TRUE!

"Women you will know. Understand them! You will not."
ABSOLUTELY TRUE!

What are my impressions from life?

First and foremost. Value Freedom. To have it is to accept
it. To lose it is to realise what it really means.

Have your opinions on matters and speak out about them.
Don't remain silent when the opportunity arises and complain
later.

Fear no man. We are all born equal.

Allow no one to look down on you or talk down to you
(unless he holds a GUN!) What have I learned from life?
It can be cruel. It can be kind. It gives you nothing except
health. It promises you death. It takes nothing from you except
years. It teaches you that what ever you get from life you must
get yourself by self education, by listening, by avoiding the
many pitfalls and by taking advantage of all or at least some of
the opportunities that exist or come your way. Take nothing for
granted at any time. It's far better to be suspicious than trustful.

I know that I have missed a number of things out of this
letter. Things that are part of my memories. Of happenings
during my life. So, if you bear with me, Dear Helen, I'll jot them
down as I might as well continue to bore you a little longer.

By the way, up to now there are over 40,000 words that
have been typed by me and of course read by you! Phew! Must
be the longest letter ever. No dim wit this fellow! After all this is
for ever and a day, for you to keep and possibly read again and
again in your latter years. For your children to read and may-be
enjoy hearing about the past.

Thoughts of my Grand-Parents are sketchy to say the least. Of course, as I said, my Father's parents were both dead long before we were born, but from photos I remember that Grand-Dad Gill was well over 6 foot tall, bearded, and very smart looking. He too was a seafarer. A Master Mariner as well as my Dad had been. He was named Francis Joseph. Where my name came from, although on my Birth Certificate I was christened Frank Joseph, so many people believe I am in fact Francis. But no! My Grand-Mother Gill, I recall was rather small. Hence my Dad being on the short side.

What of my Mother's Parents? Well, her Mother was married twice. Her first husband must have died. I don't really know. But my Mother's name was O'Reilly and her step-sister and brother were McQuirk. I do vaguely remember Grand-Mother O'Reilly. I picture her, all in black, which, in those days seemed to be the trend. Or perhaps she was mourning Grand-Father O'Reilly. I know I was very young and do not recall a lot being passed down to us over the years about them. Although I'm sure Eileen knows more than I.

Before the start of World War Two, pre 1939, I did not mention about our regular mid-night swimming that took place at the bottom of Mariners Road in Waterloo. The estuary of The River Mersey was located literally at the bottom of our road! We used to arrange to meet and a big gang, including Eileen, would be there, for a fun night. The weather then was so reliable and so hot in the summer, even at that late hour. No one needed to go abroad for sun-shine. It was always here. It's easy now to say, who has taken the Sun-Shine from our lives. After The War they did away with the popular sand-hills that formed naturally on the coastline and they also began to remove the concrete bunkers that were built to defend our beaches against the threat of enemy attack. However, even my daughters remember playing on the beach and in the obsolete structures in the mid to late 1950's and 60's! A lot of work went into building a Promenade. It took years to complete and everyone enjoyed it as they continue to do to this day. It was progress, but at this moment in time I reckon that within another few years that Prom will be no more. Why? Well the sand has been allowed to take over and it is slowly but surely covering the steps and the Promenade itself simply because they have withdrawn the labour responsible for keeping the area clear of sand and who were able to battle against the Mersey's watery skills of erosion. So much for the policy of Cut-Backs, for if they decide to rectify the problem it will cost at least ten times more than it would had they continued to employ men solely to maintain the hard work of previous Councils and their workforces. So much for progress!

I remember the time I passed my Driving Test. It was way back in the 1930's. I was then employed by Ron Panton, in Sandheys Ave, at his garage. He agreed to loan me a car. An Armstrong-Sidley. It boasted a Pre-selected gear box. That is a car where you select the gear before engaging the clutch. It had been off the road and was only completed the day before I was due my test. I drove into Liverpool city centre and, lo and behold, the vehicle broke down half way through the test. Hence my driving test had to be canceled. The second time I went I passed, so I was chuffed!

After the war I bought a motor-bike, mainly for transport to work when I was employed on the scaffolding. This was when we were living in Vermont Ave. One night Madge and I decided to go out and leave the bike at home and walk to the cinema. But we could not get in as it was house full. So we slowly wandered home. Now, on the way, I heard a motor-bike approaching and, to my astonishment, there was Jack on my bike with Mike Gilbertson on the back. They were only about fifteen years of age and, of course, no license or insurance! I waited till their return and really belted him. Lord knows what may have happened but fortunately nothing did.

During one period of my life. Yes, you guessed! When I was a POW, I became something of a expert, in my own right, in playing cards. Especially Contact-Bridge and Cribbage. YES, Cribbage! (Remember how I hammered you when playing at that hotel in Belgium,) And, of course, Patience. Cards are very like life itself. If you play them right. You win! If not. You lose and no one takes kindly to a loser.

In the early period of our marriage we used to enjoy the company of a crowd of us who used to go dancing together. There was; Gerry and Mary Murphy, John and Eileen Brown, John Mulhearn, Bill Davies, Paul Quinlin, Joe and Maisie Flood and many more. It was a smashing gang and we had fun galore. Also we arranged Bus-Trips out on Sundays. Many times John Mulhearn and I were hunting around on the Saturday night for friends to fill the coach. Jim Bremmer, the News Mag shop owner used to come with us and, prior to his death, he always spoke of the good times we had together on those outings. Talk about Tom O'Connor's comedic quip,"-Lets get out of the street chaps before we break open the beer!"--Wasn't in it! All good fun and memories to look back upon.

I remember during my life having opportunities that may have meant me being more successful than I was. First, when about seventeen, I was interviewed in Liverpool for an apprenticeship as a Van-Norman-Boring-Bar-Engineer. That was for car engine Precision Boring. I was given the job, but after some thought I decided that, as the wages were not high and with having to travel, paying fares etc, it would hardly be worth it. Perhaps a mistake, who knows?

Then, just after I was married, my Dad, who was friendly with a guy who was high up in the Royal -Liver -Insurance-Company, (it was, at that period, the trend to buy an Insurance Book and build it up over time to accumulate collateral). My Dad arranged for me to go to see this chap. A Mr Hume, at his home off Queens Drive near Liverpool City centre. I knew him for he had been to our house on occasions. Unfortunately, when I arrived, he started to condemn me for getting married when I did and suggested I should have gone on to Insurance first, established myself, then made a move to get married. Needless to say I told him a thing or two and walked out. Perhaps a mistake, who knows? But then isn't life planned out for us and really I didn't do too badly in achieveing what I did. Again, it's memories that keep cropping up you see Helen. And there's more! Come here and listen!

In the late fifties, early sixties, the Civil Defence was foremost in the plans of this country and we, in the Ambulance Service, used to have some of them coming on duty with us and accompanying us out on cases. I was not keen on that idea at all. For me it was a case of, two's company, three's a crowd and that's how it appeared when we would move cases from bedrooms etc. Many people would ask "Why are they standing there?" or "Why are they watching?"

Not a clever set up believe me. But, on the other hand, these people needed to be taught how to drive an Ambulance. They had, themselves, a real old heap of a vehicle and I was picked as one of the Instructors. This meant Saturdays and Sundays working with them to train them on our more up to date procedures. Plus evenings in the summer time taking them on the road and up to Ambulance Test standards. Of course, payment for doing the job was all part and parcel of the package. The money side of it was great for me and my family for the wages in the Ambulance Service, at that time, were notoriously low. I remember in the late 1950's early 1960's our weekly pay was 8 English pounds which transfers to round about $17! Even back then that wage was very low. Eventually this assignment stopped. I suppose it was costing too much or may be they started to trust other Nations a little more and didn't feel the need to have a Civil Defence team.

A proud time for me was when I was asked to play on the Five-A-Side football team. Because the game was so fast and because of my age, I played in goal.

When it was decided to form a league within the Ambulance Service, Skelmersdale could not raise the five needed because a number who were interested were on duty so I volunteered as a stop gap. I played a number of games and enjoyed it immensely. The Medal that was presented to me by the Five-A-Side members upon my retirement was very much appreciated and one gift that I was proud to receive.

I also have memories of the many dances that I helped to arrange with Alan Appleton and Cyril Walker while working. All were a success and much enjoyment was had by all.

As life rolls on one loses many dear friends by death. Each time it is indeed upsetting and slowly one's generation disappears to make way for another. Every time these unhappy events take place it becomes another blow to your memories. So it was that Bill Watson became ill and over a period he was up and down till in 1984 we were told by Gwen, his second wife after he and Eileen divorced, that he was deteriorating and in hospital in Canada. We decided to go over to visit him and may be help in his recovery. When we arrived it was sad to see this once, jovial, joke-telling person, in such a state. In addition to his illness, the drugs were confusing his mind and he would ramble on about all sorts.

Making sense of nothing. When one looks back to the days when all was well and you dwell upon the person in question, the way life was, the conversations, the laughter, the moments of happiness, the memories, once so real. Now so distant.

I returned to England in the September, having stayed for two months in Canada. As we parted, both Bill and I cried. For he knew and I knew, we would not meet again in this life. Poor Bill. He lasted till early December 1984. Then passed away. I regret I was not there to show my respect for him. Poor Bill. The passing of anyone is sadness and each time one feels an inward loss of part of one's own life, for these persons are the ones who built your life and living around. Mine went back to

1941 and have continued on, in an ever increasing scale since.

People who molded my character, my outlook.
Who formed the rich pattern of my life. When they die a piece
is taken away. Never to be replaced!

Madge lost her dear Mother on 6th April 1959. She too was
a great loss, for she was easy going and helped us all at periods
when everything seemed hopeless. I have some fond memories
of her.

Now Helen, if you are still with me and haven't chucked
the lot on the fire I must tell you a little more about the animals
in my life. I've told you about Peter and a little about Spot. I'll
come to him in a second. First, I vaguely recall, when we were
living in Ireland we had a big, black cat. This cat used to eat the
clothes as they were hung around the fire to dry. Needless to say,
he spent more time outside than in! It wasn't the fact that we
did not feed him! It was a case that he liked wool etc!

When living in Wallasey we got our first Pup. A wiry
little fellow that we named Bruce. Unfortunately he developed
distemper when but a few months old and died a week or so
later. What sticks in my mind was when the Bin-men came
and they took his body, tying his back legs together and hanging
him on the back of their cart. I remember Eileen and I watching
through the window with tears flooding out.

Now Spot came into our lives not long after Peter. Mum
heard of a dog having pups and Dad went to Harrington Road
close to Vermont Ave and came back with
this little black dog with a white section around one eye.
Hence the name of Spot. He was another good pal and friend.
He would sit up on the arm of my Dad's chair for hours on end.
He loved that place. I was told that, during the war years, Spot
would be laying in front of the fire, then suddenly jump up and
slowly make his way towards the kitchen and under the stairs,
where he slept and also where the rest of the family would go
during the incessant air-raids that ravaged our fair city during
the War Years. Well, some five minutes after the dog left the fire,
sure enough, the sirens would sound! Guess he could sense
what was to come.

I've told you how he welcomed me home and how he
continued to show his delight at every opportunity. After the
death of my Mother, he was, one morning laying by the fire
when all of a sudden he jumped up looking into the corner of
the room, howling and wetting himself. He then ran to the
kitchen door doing the same thing. I let him out and as the yard

door was also open, he took off. He was gone for ages. So long that I was worried and went looking for him without success. Later that evening he returned, acting really subdued. But the joy of seeing him again gave way to any thoughts of chastising him. Something had certainly spooked him that day, but we were relieved and overjoyed to see him safely home.

Some time later, as my Dad was out working and we were all away from the home, it meant Spot had either to stay in the house all day, or, if out side, remain there, waiting on the back doorstep until Dad returned home. We didn't think this arrangement was fair to the dog, so I asked Madge's Mum if she would have him. Being the kind person that she was, she agreed.Now, at this time Betty, one of Madge's sisters, was living with Grandma Prescot with her son, Lawrence. He was just a toddler, crawling around and he would get hold of Spot's flesh to stop him running away. Needless to say the dog did not like this and when I would visit the house he would go mad with joy and sit under my chair, almost pleading with me to take him out of this purgatory!, In the end I decided that it was unfair for the poor dog and possibly he would turn on the child and that would be worse. I said I would have him destroyed rather than see him so upset at what was happening. I took him out that fatal day and he must have thought his nightmare was over for he was mad with excitement! When I got to the dog's home in Brunswick Parade, Waterloo, they asked if I wanted to remain to see him put down. That was my big mistake, for I said yes. They put him in a glass cabinet and slowly the white vapour gas came in. How that dog fought to get out! In the end he just collapsed. That scene has been imprinted on my mind ever since and it upsets me every time I think of it. Perhaps thats the reason I've never had another pet? I don't know! I did a really cruel thing to that poor animal. I do know that when you lose them the sadness is so great that you wonder if the affection and love shown by the animal is really worth it.

Another mid 1980's tragedy springs to mind as I relate my more recent memories and you, Helen were there with me to witness the horror.

Liverpool football team had, once again, triumphed, in a European Championship and had reached the Final in Heysel Stadium Near Bruges, Belgium. To play an Italian team, Juventus. You were living and teaching down in London, but were in Liverpool for a half term break.

Tension and excitement were mounting in the days leading up

to the great game.

Lo and behold, we were offered tickets to this Final and, of course, we both JUMPED at the opportunity. After a few hiccups trying to get your passport sent down from London to Liverpool, we were on our Team coach and driving down south to pick up the ferry over to Belgium.

It was a festive atmosphere and such a lot of fun! Bantering with our fellow supporters and meeting new fans and old as we traveled over to Belgium on the ferry. We stayed, that first night, in a cosy hotel. The weather was very pleasant for Spring and we even sat outside, in front of the hotel reception area and played cribbage in the evening glow. That reminded me of my days as a POW as I used to while away the hours playing card games as I have mentioned before earlier in this memoir.

Our hotel was very comfortable and we were near enough to Bruges City Centre to be able to stroll around the town amid a sea of RED! Of course, there were thousands of Liverpool fans milling around. All in good humour. Though, at times, such large numbers of them, could totally dominate the city.

We laughed at some of the antics. I remember there was a famous fountain in the middle of the city and some wise guys had dressed the spouting cherub in Liverpool colours! Fans were heading into and out of local bars and cafes and generally the atmosphere and activities were innocent and in good humour. All I can say is that the Liverpool fans were just being a mass of Liverpool Fun Lovers. As usual. Certainly, no harm meant to anyone! Later that afternoon we went over to the Stadium. Right from the word go it was obvious that the whole event was an organisational NIGHTMARE!!! It was mid afternoon and the game was not due to start until later that evening. About 7pm.

There were thousands of football fans. Both from Liverpool and Italy. All milling around together. The stadium looked in pretty poor condition, even from a distance. Not the sort of standard we were used to seeing in England or at other venues we had visited in the past.

This old stadium had an outer wall but as we went to our assigned gate we were surprised to see an additional wire fence that must have been erected just for this match.

Each gate entrance at the extra fencing was manned by a number of police who were neither friendly nor helpful. No sign of the stadium personnel you would usually encounter at any game, either English or European. The police were slowly checking tickets and letting fans filter through at a snail's pace.

They were also taking any flag poles or similar items that they must have felt were potential "weapons!" Our fans were countering this by throwing their poles over the fence to retrieve once they had been admitted.

It came to our turn to  have our tickets checked. We were surprised how we were body searched by these police guys and then ordered in.

As soon as we walked into the stadium I remember turning and saying to you, "Helen. This place is crumbling and falling apart!"

Sure enough, there were chunks of concrete lying around the terraces. The concrete terraces themselves also were in pretty poor condition. Once again, there was a massive police presence within the ground. Officers with dogs who did not seem to be very friendly. Man nor Beast!

Once we began to find our bearings you asked a policeman if there were any Ladies toilets? The policeman answered gruffly and just pointed over to a circular structure that housed some urinals. You then responded and asked if there was a place for women? He, once again, indicated that this basic, outdoor and filthy place was in fact supposed to be used by both male and females for the duration of the event. Most unsanitary. Needless to say you decided to wait until after the game to find a cleaner facility!

Even at this early point we felt uneasy and uncomfortable about the whole set up. The overriding scene and atmosphere was that of a prison camp rather than a sporting venue!

There was still about four hours to go before kick off so we found standing room on the crumbling terraces and watched the stadium fill up. We were in a section located behind one of the goals. We were surprised to see that this area, set aside for the bulk of the Liverpool fans at this end of the ground, only amounted to HALF of the entire section! There was a chicken wire fence, poorly erected, which traversed the section and, at this point, was manned by a solid line of Belgium police. A wall of protection from what! On the front of all the terraces and seating surrounding the ground were high mesh fencings which had been erected in recent years in all European stadiums to stop pitch invasion and hooliganism. As time would prove, these fences only contributed to fatalities in spectators, as we all saw at Hillsborough and, that night, at Heysel Stadium. Time ticked by and many thousands of fans trickled in. It didn't take long to realise that, on our side of the makeshift fence, only Liverpool supporters were being directed and it was soon obvious that our section was becoming more and more congested and crowded with fans. A potentially dangerous situation for all those fans restricted to this area, Namely US!

The other side of the fence was also filling up but they had a lot more space to stand in and we soon realised that all these fans were actually Italian! It just didn't make sense. Why did a majority of the Liverpool fans have to be squashed into a very small section whereas the rest of the section and the ground was peopled by Juventus supporters? That meant that Liverpool supporters only had about 1/8 of the total ground capacity! Also we surmised that the other half of our section was probably full of Italians who had bought their tickets on the Black Market and for more than ticket value! There were no eating facilities at all, but we do believe that there was a hot dog vendor somewhere in our section as, after a couple of hours of waiting around and getting hungry, we were astonished to see bread rolls raining down over our heads from somewhere at the back of the section.

It was obvious what had happened. Some wise guy Scousers had realised that we were all getting hungry and that there was nowhere to buy any food, so they had waylaid the poor Vendor and commandeered his bread rolls to help out the hungry fans! Of course, this was not a good thing to do but, oh, so typical of Liverpool people and, for us, very funny! It was like manna from Heaven and we all saw the funny side of it!

Unaccountably, about two hours before the scheduled kickoff, the line of police officers manning the fence suddenly up and left, leaving just the chicken wire fence which served to separate a section of very squashed Liverpool fans and a section of predominently Italian fans who had room to move about and space to stand in! Matters were not helped by the fact that Italian fans were lobbing pieces of concrete over into our section as well as containers filled with urine. I guess we also reciprocated on that level, but such is the mentality of a huge group of fans in certain circumstances. I think it is termed "Mob Behaviour" Over a very long period of time, between two and three hours, a number of Liverpool fans on our side of the fence began to try to climb the fence to get to more space on the other side.

Of course, as more and more fans began to leave this

dangerously congested section, the flimsy fence began to fall apart and it didn't take long for the whole thing to completely collapse. At this point it was puzzling that the Belgium police did nothing to control this emerging situation! Now our supporters began to move into the other, more spacious section. At first, just a few, but as time went by and with no officials to supervise the movement, more and more of our fans were moving over the boundary to get more space. We knew that this wasn't really right of the Liverpool fans to do, but we were relieved that some of the perilous crowding was being eased and that we were getting a more fair distribution of space.

Once again. Over a very long period of time. Probably TWO HOURS! A trickle of fans on the move, became waves of hundreds of English fans, pushing into the other section and displacing the thousands of Italian fans. The Italian fans were moving over towards the side walls and trying to make way for these waves of Red football supporters. Some trapped fans were getting out of this section through the one gate way that was accessible in the front fencing. Again, The ground officials DID NOTHING to intervene in this steadily mounting situation. It was obvious that matters were becoming potentially, very dangerous, as the waves of people increased in numbers and the retreating fans were themselves becoming penned into a small side section of the terrace. Too many people were squashed into a very small area and, even at that time, there must have been many Italian fans who were sustaining injury and were having difficulty breathing!

It was at this point that it became obvious that people were in distress as the ground officials were now attempting to get people out of the congested area and onto the pitch. A difficult thing to do with only one small gate to use as an exit. All of a sudden, from our position, we saw the crowd surge over what had once been a side wall! It was obvious to us that a wall had collapsed and that many fans had been crushed! Pandemonium broke out! This was about half an hour prior to the scheduled kick off of the game. Both teams had come onto the pitch just a few minutes before this tragedy to limber up and, of course they were obliged to leave the ground in the light of this chaos. Once again, I say. This emerging tragedy could easily have been avoided if the police and ground officials had taken control in the very early stages of the incident.

We all stood and watched the horror unfold. By this time, fights and skirmishes had broken out on the stands and officials were trying to get people out of the danger area. Hundreds of people were spilling out onto the pitch. Some walking. Some crawling. Others being carried out and laid on the grass awaiting medical help.

We sat down and waited. I remember, Helen, you turning to me and saying "Dad. There are people dead down there!" I replied "No. They are not dead. They will get help!"

What else could I say? The situation was obviously very serious and there must have been fatalities, but we all needed to keep calm and get out of the danger!

Game time came and went. Ambulances and helicopters were coming and going and stretchers were being loaded onto medical vehicles and rushed to hospitals. The pitch was being used as a makeshift hospital with bodies lying all around. It was a dreadful situation!

Still time ticked by and we waited. Now, missiles were raining on us from Italian fans in connecting sections and, once again there was no police or security response! The team managers from both sides and the players came out to appeal for calm. Joe Fagin was our Manager at that time and it was obvious he was very distressed and concerned. It was a desperate situation! The situation was now in danger of spiraling out of control. Thousands of Italian fans were gagging for revenge for the casualties they could see on the field. How could anyone exit the stadium safely and calmly in the light of this riotous scenario? The Football authorities made the only choice open to them to avoid further disaster. The game would be played!

So, after about a three hour delay, this European Cup Final kicked off, to a subdued and devastated crowd. We watched the game as if in a daze and it was no surprise that we lost that game by a penalty. Later, some people would say that we had to lose the game that night otherwise there would have been even worse carnage!

I remember at Half Time, hundreds and hundreds of Juventus Supporters broke through their fencing at the other end of the pitch and started to charge across the pitch to our section, armed with whatever they could use as weapons! I even vividly remember seeing one Italian fan brandishing a fire arm that, luckily he did not use. They began to scale our fence in an attempt to get at the Liverpool fans. Our supporters were frantically shaking the fence to prevent the Juventus mob from successfully climbing into our section. In that instance the security fencing did prevent a number of our fans from being attacked and from open hand to hand fighting between both sets of fans! I still believe that there was little or no intervention from the police or ground personnel!

The second half of the game was played and at the final whistle we just wanted to be away from this disaster area. We knew that was going to be easier said than done. We were now sitting ducks as it was obvious that many Italian fans would be making their way over to our end of the pitch to wait for us to exit the ground in an attempt to get to our coaches.

As we emerged from the stadium we were bombarded with bottles and missiles of every description. I think we were lucky that it did not take us too long to locate our bus, though even when we got on the bus we were surrounded with angry crowds intent on taking out their revenge on all and any Liverpool fans who happened to be around!

As we limped through this lynch mob our driver kept stopping to let stray fans on to the bus as they were in danger of being attacked by the marauding mob!

It took a long time to get through the throng, but eventually we were able to leave the stadium area and the City and reach the safety of our hotel.

No one said a word on the journey. We were all gutted and as we began to hear on the radio, there were in fact many deaths. The final number would total forty plus! A Dark Night for football which was even further blighted by the fact that it was the Liverpool Supporters who were landed with the blame for the deaths and injuries. Our teams were also banned from playing in any European Championships for a number of years subsequently. I still say that the truth of the events of that night have never come to light and I hope that one day, some one will read this and look again at the events of that fateful night and lay the blame at the door of the Belgium officials who did NOTHING to control the thousands of fans who attended this game. In any event, that involves crowds of people, there has to be attendants and personnel who know and understand how to maintain order and safety. That did NOT happen that night and the regrettable deaths were a result of that negligence! Also to hold such an important game in such a shabby and crumbling stadium was insane! It was obviously a hazard to life and limb as was to be proved in the late afternoon and evening of that terrible day!

On our return to our hotel we all went off to our rooms.

We were emotionally and physically drained. We had no heart to discuss the shameful events of that night.

The next day we boarded our coach to take us back to the ferry and as we continued to listen to the radio reports we, even then, realised that we were the ones being blamed for the tragedy and our City, Our Country and our National Sport were going to be blighted with the blame for what had taken place. Our coach driver had talked with us as we entered the vehicle to warn us that we may be stopped en route to the ferry port as all English fans could be stopped by police and searched. Sure enough, after a short while we were pulled over and a number of police came onto our coach and searched us for, God knows what! We certainly felt as though we were the guilty parties. Lets hope that we will be vindicated in the future and that justice will be served with the truth  being investigated and our wonderful fans cleared of full responsibility.

It is now 1986.I wonder what this year holds for me? Will I make Greece and my desire to pay respect to Stan, my friend and fellow army buddy who was lost in battle in Greece. This project is very much to the fore in my mind. I have been making inquiries and hope to succeed soon in traveling over to Greece on a pilgrimage of respect to those who never returned to our shores and lost their young lives in war. What difference will this next twelve months make to my life? Will there be joy? Will there be sadness? Who knows! The future is not ours too see. Perhaps I'll add to this letter, Helen. We'll see.

Here it is. Now 1987 and I carry on to tell you just what 1986 held for me. To start with. Remember, I spoke about my desire to go and pay homage to all my lost colleagues in Greece. Well. First of all, I wrote away  to the British War Graves Commission for details of names of those whose bodies had never been found and who had their names engraved onto Memorial Stones and those comrades more fortunate, who had an actual grave and head stone. Then I bought a number of Poppy Wreaths. Also Memorial Crosses and then set about arranging the trip. I had also acquired a plan of the layout of the site at the War cemetery in Greece so I was able to plot the exact locations of the graves, etc, I wanted to honour.  It was here, Helen, that you said you would come with me to share the event and most importantly to keep me company on this sad journey to Phaleron War Cemetery  which was situated in a district just a few miles from Piraeus Harbour. Up on a beautiful, lush landscape that hugged the hills above the harbour. Your gesture was very much appreciated and I thank you most sincerely for although I've not said outwardly how much it meant to me I can assure you, dear, that to me it showed a daughters love towards her Father and I'm proud of you for that. We booked for a week if you recall, at a resort outside Athens called Rafina. A town on the east coast of the peninsula. You were teaching in London and we were able to travel in your Half Term school break in the October. We stayed in this resort that was quite a distance from Athens. The weather was perfect and we lounged around the pool and tavernas for a couple of days to prepare for our pilgrimage.

On one memorable day, we decided to explore the coastline. Helen suggested that we walk along the beach until we came across another small village. So, off we trekked. We were wearing only our swim wear and scandals, but our plan was to saunter to the next fishing town and just relax on the beach and find a small bar or restaurant to have lunch in. Off we went in the blazing midday sun.

We had been walking for about twenty minutes or so when we encountered a metal fence.

You, Helen would not be deterred by any obstacle and suggested we scale the fence in order to continue our journey. I, of course, went along with the suggestion and, with some difficulty and a sand shoe of mine lost in the surf, we were able to drop down onto the other side.

We continued our walk through, what looked like a holiday camp or hotel complex with cute little chalets and lush gardens. We were admiring the community and had decided that we must have found our selves in a working class holiday resort when we came across a large grassy square and a couple of administrative buildings. We even took photographs of each other under the impressive, towering palm trees that were slap bang in the middle of the square! Then we spotted a gateway and headed for the exit, thinking we would continue our walk into the town that must be nearby.

As we approached the gate Helen, you suddenly whispered urgently to me " Dad! Keep walking. Look straight ahead and DON'T say a word to anyone!"

Being a cooperative Father, I obeyed this command. Imagine our horror when we realised that we were walking passed TWO ARMED GUARDS posted at the gates! We silently realised that we had inadvertently strayed onto a Greek Army Base! We could easily have been arrested as spies although it would have been difficult to have hidden any sensitive documents in our swim wear! But we were taking photos on the drill field and of the Barrack Offices! It was not unheard of, at that time, for Europeans to be charged with espionage, so we could have landed ourselves in a very tricky situation!

The guards never flinched though they must have been bemused by the bikini clad, attractive young woman and an older man with only one shoe!!!

Luckily for us, before anyone realised we were trespassers of the worst kind, a local bus drove along the dusty lane. It appeared to be heading back towards our resort so we flagged it down and jumped on. We just had enough small change to pay the fares back to Rafina. Later, we laughed and laughed at our adventure and we were more than relieved that it had not resulted in a very serious situation for us.

It was on the Monday after arriving on the Saturday that we hired a car and you drove to Piraeus. You had never driven in Greece so it took a little while to become familiar with the roads and traffic signals that we had to guess at.

The first part of the journey was easy. Just head towards Athens. In those days there was no easy fix with Map Quest to guide you where ever you were in the world. We drove for quite a while until we found ourselves right in the middle of ATHENS! We knew that wasn't ultimately where we needed to be so we headed out of town on the nearest motorway and then discovered we were en route to the airport. The motorway consisted of, at least eight lanes and was heavily congested with fast moving traffic. It was time to take drastic action other wise we could have been driving aimlessly around all day and still no nearer to our destination!

Once again, Helen, you used your powers of resourcefulness and, when we stopped at the next set of traffic lights, you noticed that a taxi had pulled up in the turning lane next to us. You wound the window down and asked the taxi driver if he knew how to get to The Allied Services War Cemetery. Luckily the taxi driver spoke some English. He instantly knew where we wanted to go and, despite having a customer in the back of his cab, he motioned us to follow him. We meandered through leafy suburban streets until he dropped off his customer and then he led us further, right to the gates of the impressive memorial site.

Our first sight was most amazing! The cemetery was like a green oasis in the middle of the stark, rocky surroundings.

Obviously, lovingly tended by the gardeners and landscapers. A peaceful and poignant place of rest and reflection.

I had brought over a number of poppy wreaths and individual floral tributes and we began our Mission of Sorrow, laying each tribute on marked graves and on the huge marble slabs that were erected to honour and remember those whose bodies were never recovered. My good friend Stan Field was one of those whose only memory is a name etched in the marble. It was a bitter /sweet day. I had succeeded in my desire to pay my respects to my comrades, but, of course, the stark reality and finality of the cemetery , brought back vivid memories and emotions. We did not rush our journey through the cemetery and we were glad that we had a flask of whiskey to help numb some of the pain. At least I was able to silently let my compatriots know that they were not forgotten.

We were accompanied on most of this day trip by Brian Smith. An ex Regimental Sergent-Major from the Army-Physical-Training Company whom we had met at our hotel and who, upon hearing the reason that I was in Greece, requested to come along with us. His wife came along as well.

The visit was indeed very heart searching. The immediate entrance was the start of much sadness and much reminiscence. The thoughts of the events of that Greek Campaign, way back over 45 years ago, were relived by me. My 44l Division pals names were clearly visible on Face four of the eight Memorial Stones, containing some  2,888 names and the nine Colleagues of mine who had graves were among 2,032 buried in that War Cemetery. The Poppy Wreath I took I laid at the foot of Face 4 and the 9. Memorial crosses that I had with me were duly placed below each Head-Stone with always a short prayer and a word of greeting " HELLO DEAR-FRIEND!"

Remember Helen, how we hunted around to find those 9 graves. Going from row to row. On the Memorial Stone, clearly visible, was the name of my friend and pal, Stan Field. My peace time mate and the main reason that I made the trip. I did so want to pay respects to him. Brain Smith was so pleased that he had come along and he, like myself, was so amazed at the condition in which this Cemetery is kept. It is a credit to all concerned. So peaceful! So well maintained and I can assure all that those who gave their lives in the Greek Campaign of 1941. "DO REST IN PEACE–GOD BLESS EACH AND EVERYONE OF THEM!"

I made an Album of the Cemetery and I hope many will

view and many will remember. You Helen, took many photos and I'm sure you too were pleased that you came over with me for it was an experience never to be forgotten.

I wonder what ever happened to that Brian Smith? He was going to do all sorts if you recall. Submit an article in The British Legion News Paper. Also send on the photos that he took that day. Yet, even after I contacted him by sending a Christmas Card. Nothing! Oh well. You can't win them all! Reckon I've jumped the gun a bit, for the first important thing that happened in

1986 took place on the 9th February, for it was Madge and I's 40th Wedding Anniversary! What a surprise you girls arranged. A weekend for us all in the Cotswolds which turned out to be a wonderful few days spent together. Both your Mum and I were more than grateful for the efforts of you Helen, Triciaand Lorraine. We all, including our new and first grand daughter, Holly, had a memorable time.

Yes, 40 years, a long, long time together. We've had our ups and downs, but thank God, we are together to spend our twilight years as one and to share each additional year with happiness and memories of our life.

Later in that eventful year of 1986 a very sad event brought me much heart ache and sadness for it was on the 1st May that I lost my dear brother, Jack. He, as you know, collapsed while washing his car at home and his massive heart-attack allowed no one time to share his final breath. It was indeed a terrible blow to me for so much of my life was shared with him. He was my pal as well as my brother and his passing at 53 years of age has left a gap and a change in the events of my previous way of life.

No one knows or accepts what this loss has done to me. It always appeared that the boot would be on the other foot as the difference between our ages was something that dear Jack always feared. He worried over being left alone as he was so much younger than Eileen and I. We never considered that it would be me that had to bear the cross. He was such a respected chap. Liked by everyone. A good mixer and always ready for a laugh and joke. He has joined Mum and Dad and will look down upon us all with a desire to guide us through our remaining years.

He has left me with many, many happy events to recall, but, unfortunately they now bring tears to my eyes. We shared Friday nights out together. We shared football matches together. Our love was Liverpool Football Team and poor Jack missed our team achieving The Double. Winning both The League and The FA Cup in the same season! Beating Everton 3-1 at Wembley Stadium would have pleased him so much. I don't go out on a Friday night now, nor do I go to Anfield Football Stadium. I just can not bring myself to make the effort. Too many memories and too sad without my pal. When you come home Helen, we do go out but I know you understand how it will never be the same and I know how close you were to our Jack and how much you loved him. Poor Jack, I miss him so, so much! He was such a comedian, as most of the population of Liverpool are!

Two incidents stand out in my memory and they both concern you and ,funnily enough, FOOTBALL!

In the mid eighties, Liverpool, succeeded, once again, in qualifying for a Cup game at Wembley Stadium, our National Arena for football and located in London.

You, Helen was living and working down in "The Big Smoke"( London) at that time. Jack and I traveled to London on a club coach. We were due to meet you outside Gate H on game day as we had your ticket for the match. It was a Charity Shield game at the beginning of the season in August.

Apparently, you got to our agreed meeting place very early and waited and waited Soon the crowds converged around all the gates to gain entry and it became impossible to find each other in the swarms of fans. Needless to say, Jack and I just had to abandon any hopes of linking up with you and get to our assigned seats.

Imagine our surprise when, at the final whistle, as we were leaving our stadium section, who was waiting for us at the bottom of the stairs? YOU HELEN!

You had a few choice words for us about leaving you outside with no ticket. But you, being a resourceful Scouser and A Gill to boot, had managed to charm your self through the turnstile and into the ground just a couple of minutes into the first half! The three of us spent some time after the game laughing at the absurdity of the situation. I remember you made Jack give you his lunch sandwich as a form of recompense for abandoning you without a ticket. I think we may have sold your ticket when we couldn't find you which only fueled your wrath even more. It was certainly a most memorable moment in the lives of the two Brothers and The Daughter!

The next and most poignant occasion was our celebratory antics following Liverpool winning a European trophy in Rome.

I had traveled over to Italy to watch the amazing game and you, Helen had picked me up at the airport. We then met up with Jack in Liverpool City Centre to watch the team bring home The Cup. We had based ourselves in St Johns Precinct Car Park offices where Jack worked as a manager and then on to St Georges Hotel in the same complex. This proved a great vantage point to be able to watch the Team Bus idle it's way through the City streets. Team and Cup held aloft.

Of course, we then needed to continue our celebration so we drove back homeward, to Waterloo and based ourselves in "The Liver" pub, A bastion for all Liverpool fans. We must have first arrived there at around 6pm and decided that we would stay for just one celebratory drink. I remember you, Helen, announced that you would only stay for the one drink as you were hungry and needed to get home to have something to eat. Jack was insistent that you just have one more drink before you left. Reluctantly, you agreed. FATAL! His powers of persuasion were not to be resisted. Soon your protests changed from. "NO! I need to get home and EAT" To " Where's my next drink?"

We had such great fun that night. Every one was in party mood in the whole city and eventually, later that evening, when we three were more than ready in body to continue partying ALL NIGHT, though, in SPIRIT we were well over the top, we, very fortunately, bumped into your God Mother (Sally Feely's daughter, Barbara) with her husband, Brian in The ROYAL HOTEL BAR. They immediately realised that we three marauding drunks needed to be protected from ourselves and the community at large!

They gently persuaded us that they needed to take us home and we slurringly agreed. I think if they hadn't intervened we would have landed ourselves in some difficulties. Who knows where we would have ended up! We were transported back to our bungalow and as we were staggering into the house, Jack, who was bringing up the rear, somehow tripped and fell in the gutter, breaking his glasses and sustaining an ugly gash on his temple. He was in no fit state to be taken back to his house as his wife would have given him HELL!! Also, he had fallen into a deep sleep and really couldn't be roused.

The next question was. Who was going to phone his wife and inform her that Jack wasn't coming home that night? A daunting task for anyone! Of course it didn't take long to agree that you, Helen, should convey the bad news to his wife. With much reluctance and some trepidation, you phoned and tried to give as upbeat an explanation as possible as to why Jack would not be home that night!! Our plan worked as Eve didn't blow a gasket on the phone though we knew that once Jack got home the following day he would really be in for an interrogation session!

I remember I kept vigil next to him all that night as I was somewhat concerned that he may have sustained a concussion or some other complication from the head injury. When he awoke the next morning the first thing he said as he awakened from his sleeping place on the living room floor was."Hey Gilly! Is that picture on the wall crooked? I replied. "Yes. It is"

"Thank God for that." Said Our Jack. "I thought there was something wrong with my eyes!" We did have such fun and when he died I not only lost a brother but also a very close and cherished friend.

My birthday came, making me 67. We celebrated it, but the memories of the previous year when Jack was with us dimmed the event. Madge and I, with George and Nora Reid went, once again, for a holiday in Yugoslavia. North this time. It was just as nice as the previous year and we enjoyed it very much. As I look back over the year of 1986, a sad year I reckon, but there was one bright spot and that was having Eileen over for the Christmas. She came from Canada early December mainly to help me through that particular period of grief as she knew just what a sad time it would be without our dear brother. It was nice to have her near and as we were now but TWO, each visit is a treasured memory.

In the latter part of 1985 I started to try and trace some of my Territorial Army pals from way back in 1938. Well I did, in fact find about ten and I arranged a GET-TOGETHER in Liverpool. It was indeed a nostalgic occasion with many memories brought back to life. We've had a few meetings since and a number of us have joined the Royal Engineers Association at Fazakerley and meet once a month so, keeping in touch with each other.

Baby Holly continues to grow up and is really beautiful. Good health has favoured us all in 1986. Thank God, and with that I say good-bye to 1986 and hello to 1987, again asking the question."WHAT DOES IT HOLD?" I know that in March Patricia is due another Baby giving us our second Grand-Child. That will be a happy event.

Then, in late July Helen and Peter are due to get married.

Another happy event within the family. The rest of the year is WAIT AND SEE.

Well Dear Helen, here it is now, drawing to the close of 1987 and before I finish this letter to you I must say a little about this year for the events that took place are most important to me. It was on the 24th March that Kyle, our first Grand Son was born. This little fellow is a Smasher and growing into a real lad!

Both your Mum and I are made up with both our Grand Children, as is expected. How pleased we all were that everything this time was alright and no worries as in the case of Holly. Only a couple of hours after she was born in a London hospital, she was whisked off to Great Ormand Street Childrens' Specialist Hospital in Central London as it appeared that she may have had a very serious medical condition. Poor Trish and Cathal were in shock. A new baby who was snatched away from them and put in an incubator for days. Initially Cathal had accompanied the infant in the ambulance to the specialist unit. Poor Tricia was left with only a Polaroid snapshot of her new child. She was left in a side ward without much information and just a load of anguish, not knowing what was happening. At least you were there Helen to help to comfort and support her and be her voice to the medical staff. At long last she was discharged from the initial hospital and you were able to drive her across town to stand vigil next to Holly's incubator for a number of days. How awful that she was unable to hug her new born. Only look on at a tiny person all hooked up with various tubes and respirators. Thank God that the outcome was favourable. There was no medical condition and Mother and Baby were reunited. Quite a terrible trauma for Tricia to begin her days as a mother.

You know Helen, many times over the past years you and I have stood side by side, especially for such events as; Parachuting, Gliding, Scuba Diving, watching Liverpool Football Team. Standing together on the famous "Kop" where all the true Liverpool football supporters stand and cheer, going overseas to watch them and most important our trip to Greece. All has made me very proud but on Friday the 31st July 1987, when I was again by your side, was, with out doubt, the proudest time of them all! For you were very, very happy, and so was I. It was your most important day and you looked beautiful. And I was YOUR Dad! Taking you to the Church to complete your dream of becoming the wife of Peter. Sharing life as one, and sharing the most important thing in this life, Love.

If you recall earlier in this letter, I said that I wanted to see both you and Lorraine, married and settled like Patricia. Well, Thank God it has come true in your case. Now we await upon Lorraine. Who knows what 1988 may bring? Again Helen I must say how really proud I was on your Wedding Day and the memory of your joy will for ever be imprinted in my mind. God Bless You And Keep You Safe For Ever.

Our 41st Anniversary came and went with a speedy regularity. As if the 40th had been only the week before. 1988 will see 42 years. Wonder if we'll reach 50? Who knows! My 68th Birthday was celebrated close to the place of my 66th What a difference those two years have made. This time it was Eileen who was with us and I suppose I should be thankful for that. Can't think of any more to say, so perhaps I should close this special long, long letter to you, Helen and if it takes you as long to read it as it has taken me to type it, you will be approaching 1989.

I'll say good-bye now, Dear Helen. All my love to you. Take care and retain this letter always. Bless you and thank you so much for being a lovely, loving daughter.

Your Ever Loving Dad.
xxx-xxx.

P.s.
Much joy, happiness and love, to you Helen and Peter in your first house together. 18th December 1987. XX

## Chapter 18
# Update 2008

Since finishing this wonderful life account in the mid 1980's my Dad, Frank Gill has gone from strength to strength in all he has achieved and he has worked diligently and sincerely to help those around him to always get a fair deal in life. He has now reached the golden age of 88 and is still as vibrant, sharp and involved as he was in all his previous years on this earth.

After writing this documentary on his life experiences, he then went on to become committed to a number of local and national organisations where he has made a huge impact on their foundation and development. So that today there are well established and strong associations that represent groups of people from many walks of life. Always striving to help his fellow working man to achieve their rights at whatever age they may be.

He has been an important influence in setting up "The Retired Ambulance mans' Association". A much needed support group for personnel of all ages who may have had to retire early due to work related illness or injury as well as the many older staff who retire at the ages of 60 or 65. His tireless efforts to bring this group of people into high profile with the main ambulance hierarchy has served to highlight and help many who otherwise may have been overlooked by their working counterparts. Frank has worked as Secretary and, later, as President of this worthwhile cause.

Another association he has been closely linked with and has had a great influence on is "The Royal Engineers." His involvement to this group, of course, dates back to his army days and reflects his strong loyalty and sincere commitment to all and everything he comes into contact with. His efforts to always keep an organisation moving forward and gaining strength for the benefit of it's members is remarkable.

After his pilgrimage over to Greece to honour his "Fallen Friends and Compatriots", he became passionately committed to a small association called "The Greek Veterans." He and Ed Horlington, a great friend and colleague in this venture, established and developed a wonderful social and lobbying group who would travel to Kalamata annually to meet and reminisce and honour their comrades. Survivors and deceased, in this small, southerly Greek City which in the early 1940s had been like a "Mediterranean Dunkirk" with many Allied troops escaping from these Greek shores to go on to be posted to Burma etc. and who even became POWS of the Japanese. Definitely "from the frying pan into the fire"

Wonderful May times in Kalamata when, each year, more and more links to the past would surface.

I will always remember the local lady, who attended one of the first Memorial Services held in the Park in the centre of Kalamata. She had been a member of The Greek Underground during The Second World War and had aided many frightened and fleeing Allied troops to avoid capture by the Germans and to make their escape to Crete. After 50 years she was able to " Come down from the Greek hills" and meet again these admirable lads who had fought so hard to help her people. Of course my Dad, Frank, never made it that far south in Greece to attempt a getaway, but imagine the marvel and awe of being able to return regularly to Southern Greece and to be able to discover and put into place more puzzle pieces that would provide such a detailed insight into those nightmare War years. "The Greek Veterans", over the years have achieved many wonderful and lasting things that will eternally pay homage to all those Brave and Courageous Heroes of The Greek Campaign 1940-1941. Not a very lengthy campaign, but certainly vitally important in the events of "The Second World War"

A permanent Memorial Stone and garden has been erected in The Kalamata Park and many local dignitaries have become involved , appreciative and committed to this group. One of the most significant achievements that Frank and Ed have been such an important influence is their incessant lobbying of the British Military Authorities to actually be awarded A MEDAL for their involvement in "The Greek Campaign." For many years this "Quiet Campaign " was kept under wraps by The British Government as the troops had been sent into a place where it was a no-win situation. The German foe had already occupied Greece and British soldiers like Frank were sent in with the knowledge that they would not make any impact! Almost like sacrificial lambs to the slaughter, but that's what war is all about.

Victims on all sides, at all times! Pawns in a military game!

Imagine the sense of achievement and justice when, at long, long last, "The Greek Campaign" medals came through and The Guys had their official recognition for the ordeal that they had endured for their country and for the youth that they had lost in these endeavors.

"The Greek veterans" have achieved amazing things. In the Midlands There is now a Greek Arboretum in "The Memorial Gardens for The World War Two Campaigns" and this peaceful and reflective area would certainly not be in existence if it wasn't for the efforts of Frank and Ed.

No venture was regarded as impossible or unsolvable. They knew what was right and they would not be deterred by bureaucracy or any red tape! The result of their David and Goliath efforts has resulted in permanent and lasting tributes to their lives and hearts and to the continuing memories of their comrades who had no voice and whose lives were cut so tragically short on the fields of war.

This publication has been read by many people, on both sides of The Atlantic and is a wonderful testament to the spirit and strength of Frank, My Dad.

I would estimate that around 300 people have read and enjoyed this insight into the life and thoughts of a Twentieth Century man who survived war and incarceration to emerge intact as a free spirit. An exuberance for the important things in life that could never be stifled or dampened , even under such barbaric and heartless treatment.

Love you forever dad. Thanks so much for giving me your life to treasure

Your Loving Daughter

Helen

22  CROSBY HERALD, Thursday, October 17, 2002

LOCAL HISTO

MEMORIES ● (Above) Head of the local history unit Mark Sargant welcomes Frank Gill to Crosby Library.  Code SJ230802K

I must confess, the first time you gave me your fathers book (3 or 4 years ago), I skimmed through it not having much time to read it at length.

Tonight I put the manuscript into type and as I was formatting it, I started re-reading it. This time I couldn't stop reading it! It was so well written from the heart. And your fathers private observations were so touching and so impactful. It took me twice as long to set the type because I just couldn't stop reading it from start to finish, as I worked. Everyone should read this to gain an appreciation for the sacrifices made by this "Greatest Generation". Despite what he writes to the contrary, your father really is a hero who came face to face with tyranny and spat at it. Just unbelievable courage. And his homecoming was so terribly bittersweet.

Randy Rhinesmith, Hotbutton Creative                January 4, 2008

16597986R00107

Printed in Great Britain
by Amazon